Suffolk
Arts an

You may
for retur
Providing it has not
you may renew it, e
by post-quoting the it
number, name, a
Unfortunately, items cannot by renewed by telephone.

CW00431366

20/7/00

COUNTY

RESERVE

10 J

2014

1 5 SEP 2023

Any overdue charges on this item will be made at the current
ADULT rate.

6 week loan

30127 05746076 3

STEVIE WONDER

Stevie Wonder is unique. He is not just a musician, he is a composer, arranger, producer, multi-instrumentalist and singer of outstanding brilliance. Despite the handicap of his blindness and his background of poverty he has become one of the most highly acclaimed and consistently popular superstars of rock music. After amazing recording sucesses in his teens, he managed to free himself from record company restrictions to develop his own musical style, which has been immensely influential. This is the story of both his life and his music.

STEVIE WONDER

Ray Fox Cumming

MANDABROOK BOOKS

First published in Great Britain by
Mandabrook Ltd, 1977

Copyright © Mandabrook Ltd

Printed in Great Britain by
Richard Clay (The Chaucer Press) Ltd
Bungay, Suffolk

ISBN 0 427 00418 7

FOREWORD

This book is not a personal appraisal of the life and work of Stevie Wonder. It is rather a documentary account of his growth from child genius in a lower-middle class Detroit family to one of the greatest superstars contemporary music has known.

The opinions expressed in this book are those of many people – Stevie's friends, family, people he has worked with, and many journalists. I am particularly indebted to the writers from whose articles I have quoted, and who are in most cases credited by name.

RAY FOX-CUMMING, 1977

CHAPTER ONE

Stevie Wonder was born on May 13th, 1950, under the sign of Taurus, a fact which he thinks highly significant. He is a firm believer in astrology and considers himself to be a very proper Taurean. His pride in his birth sign has been publicised in his business activities. One of his companies had 'Taurus' in its title, another 'black bull'.

He also feels that aspects of his birth sign have a direct affect on his life. For example, when his marriage to Syreeta Wright broke up, he put its failure down to 'Taureans and Leos finding it hard to live together, being both such strong characters'.

There are now hundreds of books available analysing the different signs of the zodiac and their characteristics. The vices and virtues which they attribute to people born under the different birth signs vary widely and often directly contradict each other, but perhaps the best and most concise description of a Taurus is one written by a British astrologer centuries ago that still holds good today. It states:

TAURUS THE BULL
Planet Venus
Dates April 21st to May 20th
Colour Blue
Stones Lapis Lazuli and Turquoise
Element Earth

Friends Virgo and Capricorn

Enemies Leo and Aquarius. Scorpio is a most terribl enemy if of the same sex, but they may yet be successfull united in marriage.

Occupations Caring greatly for money, a banker, pawn broker, a secondhand dealer. Or having great affinity wit the Earth or the land, but no skill with edged tools, mayb a farmer, gardener, builder or architect.

If born with stars well placed Quiet and pleasant, no given to law, quarrell, or wrangling, not vicious. Neat spruce and loving. Mirth in words and actions. Cleanly i apparel. Rather drinking much than gluttonous, prone to venery, oft entangled in love matters, zealous in affections Musicall, and they shall be singers with sweet pleasan voices, delighting in baths and all honest merry meetings or maskes or stage playes. Easie of beliefe and not taken to labour or take any pains, a company keeper, cheerful nothing mistrustful. Right virtuous, oft had in some jealousy yet no cause for it. They shall love flowers and sweet smells, and shall be liberal to their friends.

If stars ill-placed Riotous, expensive, wholly given to looseness and lewd companies of women, nothing regarding their reputation, coveting unlawful beds. Incestuous, an adulterer, fantastical, a mere skipjack, of no faith, no repute, no credit, spending their means in ale houses, tavernes and amongst scandalous, loose people.

If Stevie had heeded what the ancient astrologer had to say about enemies, he would have known in advance that he was asking for trouble by marrying a Leo, but the occupation section of the stargazer's predictions seems not to apply to Stevie. Although he has amassed a great deal of money during his career, he certainly has no obsession with it. His own lifestyle is simple and a great deal of his wealth has gone to help people in need. He does, however, have an affinity with the land and claims to appreciate the beauties of the world, even though he is blind, a lot better than some people with perfect vision. It is impossible to speculate on whether Stevie has or has not any skill with 'edged tools', because he's never been called on to hoe or scythe and probably prefers to wield an electric razor rather than a wet shaver, which is probably the nearest thing to an edged tool that a modern city dweller ever gets to use!

Stevie may not conform with a Taurean's proper occupation, but he measures up well to the typical Taurean with 'stars well placed'. He is certainly quiet and pleasant in manner, not given to legal wranglings and is neat, spruce and loving. The 'mirth in words and actions' most definitely applies and in the course of this book there will be many references to his ready sense of humour and fun.

He is neither an over-eater nor a heavy boozer. His thinness is evidence of the former and he has often said that he doesn't need drink or drugs; he is already high on just living.

Perhaps the less said about 'oft entangled in love matters' the better!

'Musicall and they shall be singers with sweet pleasant voices' could have been written for Stevie. Obviously it applies. Throughout history there have been many notable Taurean musicians, including Tchaikovsky, Irving Berlin, Richard D'Oyly Carte (founder of the opera company of the same name), conductor Sir Thomas Beecham and violinist Yehudi Menuhin. Other famous, or infamous, Taureans include William Shakespeare, Mussolini, Leonardo Da Vinci, Napoleon and Dame Margot Fonteyn.

9

It is not true that Stevie is 'not taken to labour or take any pains', because he is a hard-working perfectionist, but he can accurately be described as 'a company keeper cheerful' and 'nothing mistrustful'.

Stevie is one of those typical Taureans who are 'liberal to their friends'. His generosity to his family, close associates and people who are worse off than himself is one of his most endearing characteristics.

Stevie's stars are without doubt 'well placed' for none of the faults attributed to the hapless ill-starred Taurean apply to him.

By and large Stevie Wonder is a typical Taurean. The Taurus musicality is, obviously, developed in him to an exceptional degree, and he has the sign's sunny disposition and generosity of thought and deed.

He has in his nature none of the fatal flaws which have wrecked the lives and careers of so many famous musicians and his story is one of continuing progress and achievement.

He is now twenty-seven years old and has been a recording artist for fifteen years. The most amazing feature of his career is that, labelled a genius at the tender age of twelve, he has consistently managed with each new recording and each new tour to top all his previous accomplishments.

Many people felt that Stevie, like many other precocious child talents, would burn himself out before he ever reached adulthood, but quite the reverse happened. In commercial terms, however, he has not always been successful and it is to his credit that, during times when he was exploring new directions and suffering from doing so with reduced record sales, he would always stick to his guns and pursue his course until the public caught up with him.

Most artists on the Tamla Motown label have always been subjected to a certain amount of control regarding their musical direction, but Stevie earned such respect from Motown that he was allowed to cut free and mastermind his own musical policy – even if he did have to fight to do it.

Perhaps the greatest achievement of his career has been that he has managed to become more than just a black performer of black music. He has been associated with every kind of modern music from soul to rock to jazz to middle-of-the-road ballads and he has become a consummate artist in every field.

People have long stopped categorising him, knowing that it would be foolish to try. His talent embraces all kinds of music and even the most sceptical of critics would not gibe at the term 'genius' being applied to him.

This book is primarily the story of Stevie Wonder as a musician – singer, instrumentalist, composer, performer and producer. It is also the story of Stevie as a person, his likes, his dislikes, and the things he feels, but it will make no attempt to delve into his private life, because that is something that he has always preferred to keep private and it is a privacy that should be respected.

One of the most amazing aspects of Stevie's life is how little it has been affected by his blindness.

He has been blind since birth and repeatedly says, 'It ain't no handicap to me.' At first one might think that he is just putting a brave face on things, but in the end you come to realise that he really does mean it.

Being blind never prevented him as a child from playing just like any other child and getting into just as much mischief. It did not prevent him from learning to play harmonica, piano, drums and later on mastering the complexities of synthesisers.

Like many blind people, Stevie has developed an exceptional sense of hearing, which helps partially to make up for his lack of sight, and his vivid imagination has provided him with mind pictures of everything that is happening in the world around him.

'There's no need to feel sorry for me,' Stevie said on one occasion. 'I'm all right. The people I feel sorry for are those who have sight but still don't see.'

CHAPTER TWO

There has always been a great deal of confusion about Stevie Wonder's real name, to the stage where an official British Motown biography inexcusably pronounced that his Christian name was Steven, when in fact it was, and always has been, Stevland.

He was the third of six children born to his mother by different fathers. Stevie's father's name was Judkins, but the name of another man named Morris was put on his birth certificate, and Stevland Morris was the name Stevie used to sign his first contract with Motown. His stepfather's name, however, was Hardaway and at some point in his early life he was known by that name.

Stevie Wonder was the name chosen for Stevland by Berry Gordy, top man at Motown, who was not hard put to think of it since Stevie was already being referred to as 'the boy wonder' around the studios.

Of Stevie's brothers and sister, Timothy and Calvin were older, Milton, Larry and Renee younger.

Stevie was born in the town of Saginaw, Michigan, but when he was still very young the family moved to Detroit where Mr Hardaway worked as a baker. The family lived a lower-middle class black style of life and were always short of money.

'When I was young,' he recalls, 'my mother, my brothers and I had to go on this drydock where there was coal and steal some to keep us warm. To a poor person that is not stealing, that is not a crime, it's a necessity.'

Stevie's mother, Mrs Lulu Hardaway, has said that she had always hoped for a musician in her family.

'So God blessed me with Steve,' she said, with emotion in her voice, 'and I didn't know that he would take his eyesight for the gift, for music. It really did hurt me. But God have blessed me. He have blessed Steve. He have blessed the whole family and I'm really happy. And Steve have been a wonderful child in my life.'

Steve's family obviously realised that he was blind before he did. 'I didn't realise that one of my senses was missing until I was four and I got punished for stepping in dog muck in my back yard. I knew something was wrong, but I didn't even react to it except I knew I got a whuppin'.'

The Hardaways made a policy of treating Steve as far as possible like any of their other children. When the brothers were caught scrumping apples from someone else's garden, he got a 'whuppin'' just like the others.

'It hurt all right,' he says, with a laugh at the recollection, 'because they'd use an ironing cord to whupp us with.'

Steve as a child managed to get into just as much mischief as his brothers, often even more so. He was frequently caught, by horrified relatives, leaping with his brothers from one shed roof to the next over a drop of twelve feet or more. Somehow he never had a bad fall.

Another favourite game was to find old car wheels and whizz them down steep hills. Steve might not be able to see where the wheel was going, but he certainly enjoyed the sound of the crash when something brought it to a halt.

Later on, Steve was not slow in discovering the opposite sex. The favourite place for conducting adolescent romantic experiments was down by the railway tracks nearby and Steve, by all reports, did not have much trouble in finding either the girls or the railway tracks!

Once Steve had figured out that he was blind, he had no trouble in coming to terms with the fact, and throughout his life he has repeatedly said that he finds it no handicap. Others, however, thought differently. When he was still a young boy living in Detroit, his mother, at the instigation of her friends, took him to a succession of faith-healers to try and 'cure' his blindness. These quacks, invoking the power of God, would murmur chants over him, mumble prayers over him, and urge him to have a courage and confidence. Then they would seize him dramatically by the shoulders or lay their hands on his eyes, so that the power of the Lord could flow through them, and then order him to see. Congenital blindness, they maintained, was a disease and an affliction which should not merely be adjusted to or accepted, but must be cast out altogether.

Of course it was an unnecessary, harrowing experience for the child in question, but anxious parents can often easily be coaxed into trying anything. Stevie, thankfully, was quite unaffected by it all. He did not go along with the disease idea and couldn't figure out what all the fuss was about, but for a less well-adjusted child, the effects could have been frightening.

On the face of it, the future did not hold much promise for a lower-class blind and black boy from the big motor town. He could have ended up making brooms, pencils or macramé flowerpot holders or, worse still, hanging round street corners with a guide dog or maybe stumbling round the city with a harmonica in one hand and a begging bowl in the other.

But little boys don't think much about the future and

Stevie was no exception. He was out to enjoy himself and got up to enough pranks to make sure that he did. Apart from getting into mischief with other lads in the neighbourhood, however, he was good at making entertainment for himself. Even as a very small child he was crazy about music. 'Pledging My Love' by Johnny Ace is the first song he can remember, but soon he was in to all sorts of things – Chuck Willis, Jackie Wilson, Ray Charles, La Verne Baker, The Drifters, Clyde MaPhatter, The Miracles, Neil Sedaka, Paul Anka, Del Shannon, The Big Bopper ... a wide, wide variety of people.

And he was making music himself. An uncle, who was a barber, knew that the little blind kid was mad about music and presented him with a four hole harmonica on a chain, so as he could wear it round his neck and not lose it.

To Stevie, it was the best present anyone could have. He started off teaching himself bits of hornpipes which people would whistle for him, snatches of which were later to appear on 'Fingertips', his first big US hit. Then he graduated to copping solos off records on the radio, adapting them for his four hole harmonica as best he could.

Soon after he had mastered the rudiments of the harmonica, Stevie was given a set of tin drums with cardboard tops as a Christmas present. Within weeks he had hammered hell out of them and rendered them completely useless. After that a new set of tin drums became a standard present every Christmas and birthday until the local Lions club eventually bought him a proper set of drums.

Christmas was one of the few times that Stevie was conscious of his blindness. 'I'd meet friends after Christmas and they would show me their presents and say, "Look what I've got," and of course I didn't know what it was they were showing me.'

Once Stevie had got the hang of his drums, he also acquired some bongos and then, when he was seven, a piano arrived. It belonged to a friendly neighbour, who was moving away from the district and couldn't take it with her, so she left it for Stevie to have.

'I was terribly excited,' he recalls. 'I kept pestering my mother, asking when it was going to arrive. I never realised at the time though just how important that piano was going to be to me.'

Apart from his family and his music, the church was a big influence in Stevie's early life. He was a junior deacon at the ultra-puritan black church in Detroit, the White-stone Baptist Church. 'I had visions of becoming a minister,' he often says, 'but in the end I decided to be a sinner instead!'

There is some confusion about how Stevie first went to Motown, although there is no doubt that it was Ronnie White of the Miracles who took him there.

Most reports claim that Stevie first went to Motown when he was eleven and was marched straight in to meet Berry Gordy, but actually it did not happen like that.

He first went to the Hitsville Studios (Hitsville being the company Berry Gordy operated before he formed Motown) when he was nine.

Clarence Paul, Stevie's long-time musical conductor and friend, says candidly, 'He was an absolute pest. He'd come by at three o'clock every afternoon after school and stay until dark. He'd play every instrument in the place and bust in on you when you were cuttin' someone else's record.'

Stevie managed to get Ronnie White to take him to the studios, because Ronnie was the elder brother of one of

Stevie's playmates. Ronnie had been told about Stevie by his kid brother, was fascinated and went along to see Stevie at his home. He was so impressed with the boy's dexterity on harmonica, piano, drums and bongos that he took him along to meet people at the studio. And once Stevie had got inside the place, nothing was going to stop him returning there every day.

Clarence may have found the little blind boy a bit of a nuisance to have around the place, but he was as impressed with his talent as Ronnie White had been.

People around the studio called Stevie the little boy wonder and Clarence called him little Stevie, so, by the time he was taken to meet Berry Gordy, his new name was just about obvious.

In 1961, when he was eleven, Stevie was finally taken to meet Berry Gordy and record producer Brian Holland. Both were immediately impressed by Stevie's talent and he was offered a long-term contract on the spot. Little Stevie Wonder was on his way.

CHAPTER THREE

tevie ceased to be 'little' in the summer of 1964 when the
ag was dropped from his name for the release of his
ingle, 'Hey Harmonica Man'. It heralded the beginning
f his maturity, his passing from boyhood into manhood.
n the early part of 1964 his voice broke and if there were
ny qualms about whether his new voice would still be
hat of a singer, they were never expressed. It all hap-
ened quickly and without fuss and there was no discern-
ble pause in his record output.

'We had more than enough recordings in the can to
ide us over the months while my voice was breaking,' he
aid later.

Almost as soon as he was physically capable of doing so,
tevie sprouted a moustache, no mere wisp of bum fluff,
ut a neatly trimmed growth of which any fifteen-year-old
ould be justly proud.

As if not wishing to be ashamed of its hairy addition,
tevie's face began to lose its babyish look and he ap-
eared, for all the world, like a gangly young hopeful for
 major basketball team.

He was also maturing as a composer. On and off he had
vritten bits and pieces, with which he was credited on
is records, but it wasn't until 'Uptight (Everything's Al-
ight)' that he made his first major contribution as a
writer. It was released in America towards the end of
965 and soon shot to number three in the *Billboard* Hot

100. Release in Britain followed in January 1966 and perhaps aided by Stevie's visit to Britain for a one-nighter tour, it strode into the UK charts, peaking at number fourteen. It was his first major British hit.

'Uptight' was a spunky, dynamic record and very much in tune with what Motown were putting out at the time. Stevie himself said his surroundings had a lot to do with the way he wrote songs, particularly at that time. 'With that song I wrote the music and the melody and then came up with the punchline "Baby, everything's alright uptight, out of sight".'

The rest of the lyrics were written by Henry Cosby and Sylvia Moy and thus began Stevie's practice of composing in association with a succession of different lyricists.

Songwriting has always come easily to him. As a staff writer of the Detroit free press observed back in 1965, 'He can invent a tune one day, brush his teeth for ten more days without humming it again, and then nonchalantly remember and commit the notes to tape.'

By the time Stevie had reached the age of fifteen, people at the Motown Record Corporation were getting decidedly nervous. The little boy whom they had taken on and steered along a successful, if predictable, course had suddenly grown up and was likely to be more tricky to handle in his late teens than he had been in his early adolescence. Not because of any temperament problems, since they knew Stevie wasn't the kind of guy prone to throw artistic moodies, but simply because his potential had become so much greater. The rewards might be higher, but the pitfalls all the more alarming and the transition from childhood star to adult performer is an operation not easily undertaken. Many young hopefuls have failed to make that awkward leap.

Stevie himself seemed undaunted by it all. Perhaps he

was unaware that anything could go wrong, but at any rate his good humour, natural buoyancy and enthusiasm never seemed to desert him. Even though he could not see his audiences, he seemed to have some kind of sixth sense which enabled him to sense their mood and strike up an instant rapport. As he stood in the wings waiting to go on, he would say to anyone within earshot, 'I wonder, how will these cats swing here?' It was more a way of issuing a challenge to himself and getting his adrenalin going than a real worry.

When he went out on one of the Motown tours, it was not just his drums and harmonica that went with him. He was still of school age and carted enough educational material around to equip a whole class. Often he would hike his luggage round himself and once, because he walked into a plush hotel carrying a formidable amount of baggage, his fans waiting outside mistook him for the bellhop and failed to recognise him.

With Stevie on tour went a young teacher, named Ted Hull, who had been specially trained in teaching the blind and who, for a while, doubled as Stevie's business manager. Among their equipment were four text books in ordinary print, five books in braille, a cue board for arithmetic, a tape recorder, a typewriter, a braille writer, a special slate and pen for braille writing, a talking book machine and talking books from the library as well as the usual paper, pencils and so on.

Stevie was an assiduous reader, who seemed to be more interested in either the past or the future than the present. He was keenly interested in the history of different civilizations, their roots and their development, but was also an avid follower of writers who dealt with space or the future.

One book that made a deep impression on Stevie in his

teens was George Orwell's *1984*, much later the inspiration for one of his songs. Perhaps that book contributed to Stevie's pessimism over the world's future, a subject which he often mentions when prompted. It's his view that the end of the world is not that many years off.

In his schooling, Stevie was well ahead of most other blind students in many areas, although his spelling was atrocious and his maths left much to be desired. In general though he was a quick learner and well ahead of what might have been expected.

'It isn't really that we go so fast though,' his teacher explained. 'It's just that the others have to go slower. For instance, in one week when the youngsters at the Michigan State School for the Blind had only two and a half days of classes because of a National Association convention, Stevie and I worked five full school days.'

Stevie would spend roughly half of the year on tour with his tutor providing his education, but for the rest of the time he would be at school in Lansing, Michigan, living in with around 265 other blind boys and girls.

In the months he spent at school, Stevie was already preparing for his future. He took the trouble to learn braille musical symbols so that one day he would be able to do his own arranging. At this time, however, music was not the only career he saw as a possibility for the future. 'I was always very interested in electrical things and felt that I might like to go to college and major in electronics. Fortunately it didn't take me long to realise that for someone who was blind, this was totally impractical. I could have blown everybody up!'

When he was at home with his family, he was quite self-disciplined about homework. Sometimes he would disappear off down into the basement to avoid being distracted by his brothers and sister, while at other times he would work at the kitchen table with one hand permanently delving into the cereal packet.

Even in his mid-teens he refused to allow himself to be incapacitated by his blindness. He would move quickly about rooms that he knew, taking the steps up to his home two at a time. In strange places he would insist on working out the layout for himself, laughing as he stumbled against unfamiliar furniture.

By now his character was already well developed. He had enormous personal charm and was well liked by everybody he came into contact with. He seemed always to be cheerful and in a happy state of mind, without at the same time being happy-go-lucky. He was professional as well as enthusiastic towards his musical commitments and made no attempt to shirk his schoolwork, even the subjects he liked least. Whatever he was doing, he was always mentally fully alert, partly because he slept soundly for eight or nine hours per night and partly because pressures were not allowed to build up to an extent where they might begin to sap his energy.

As Ted Hull explained at the time, 'Stevie aims to get to bed after a show by midnight and if he does, then we're up and at studies by nine in the morning, working through to twelve. If things get too hectic, I call the office and say, "We have to slack up on the shows now, because we're getting behind in our work."'

After the official three-hour school session in the morning, Stevie would find odd moments to study later in the course of the day. 'In show business,' he said, 'you're not really doing anything for a lot of the time. You're waiting for a guy to tell you to do something and that's when I try to read books.'

On tour abroad he would get the people he met to help him with social studies projects set for him by Ted.

'While we were in Europe on tour last year,' Ted said in '65, 'Stevie, armed with a tape recorder, would ask questions of performers and journalists he met about the racial situation prevailing in whatever particular country we were in and, in Britain, he was particularly interested to learn about the class structure.'

Ted was concerned mostly that Stevie's lessons should be of practical use to him. Reading and music reading in braille were given top priority while little importance was placed on writing.

'I taught him little more in that direction than how to write his name. He normally signed autographs in braille. When someone insisted on an ordinary signature instead, I would take his hand and help him, because, when a crowd was jostling him, he would find it difficult.'

Stevie's lifestyle has never been extravagant, but in his teenage years it could not have been. Although he was earning a lot of money, he did not have the use of it. All his earnings were sunk into a federally operated trust fund, and administered scrupulously in his best interests so that when he came of age, his earnings as a minor would not only be intact but increased by wise investment. There was certainly no question of anyone ever taking advantage of his youth and misappropriating his money. When, on attaining majority, the trust fund was handed over to him, Stevie expressed both admiration and gratitude for the way in which his affairs had been handled.

At the age of fifteen, however, he was seeing no money apart from an allowance of two dollars fifty cents a week (about a pound in those days) which would not have been considered over-generous by the parents of any American boy.

He would have liked to have used some of his wealth to

buy presents for his family, to whom he was later to show great generosity as his thankyou for all they had done for him, but the trust fund did not provide for money to be used for this purpose and, at this time, the family home did not even boast a fridge.

Stevie was fond of his home and towards the end of a long tour would begin to long to return there. When he was at an airport waiting to fly home after one tour, somebody quipped to him, 'You won't need your white stick cane today, Stevie. I reckon the pull of home will suck you into the plane!'

At this time, Motown artists always dressed smartly on stage and Stevie was no exception. He would generally wear an evening suit, either black or white, of silken or other very expensive material with a dress shirt, often with lace and a bow tie. Pictures of him working in the studio in those days show him looking only slightly less formal. While his backing musicians play in sweaters or knitted shirts, Stevie's kitted out in a dark suit, white shirt and plain narrow tie. In 1965, flower power and the kipper tie, which was the first hint of everything getting wider, floppier and dissolving into shapelessness, had not yet arrived. Even the Rolling Stones were still as often as not seen in tab-collared shirts and ties.

By 1965, Stevie's fourth year with Motown, he had covered, in recordings and concerts, a wide range of styles, from the brilliant to the ludicrous and from jazz to middle-of-the-road to whipped-up disco funk.

Stevie's early records were mostly written by Henry Cosby and Clarence Paul and his first ever recording was a diluted version of Clarence's 'You Made A Vow', tweely renamed by Motown 'Mother Thank You'. 'They [Motown] thought that [the original title] was too lovey for me, too adult,' Stevie told *Rolling Stones* later.

A couple of forgettable singles followed for America in '62 before 'Contract Of Love' came out on Boxing Day at the end of that year. It was a heavily arranged number which owed more than a little to the Four Seasons hit 'Big Girls Don't Cry', but, as Stevie says, 'it made a little noise in the sales ratings', and hinted at better and greater things to come.

Lyrically, 'Contract Of Love' was scarcely suitable for Stevie then, since here were lines like 'I've loved and lost so many times before' being sung in the high-pitched voice of a mere twelve-year-old.

At the end of 1962, Berry Gordy, label boss of Tamla Motown, was still firmly convinced that in Stevie he had a child genius, but the boy now had a handful of singles behind him, all of which had scarcely paid their way and, for a new label, this was simply not viable and could not continue. The time had come to think seriously about how the youngster's talents could best be showcased to get him across to a mass audience.

Gordy hit upon the idea of recording the boy live in concert, when surely he would be able to capture Stevie's natural exuberance. The venture, however, was not without problems. Since Stevie was too young to be allowed by the law to play clubs, a suitable theatre venue had to be found instead. Finding the right one took some time, but eventually Gordy opted for the Apollo Theatre in Harlem, famed black area of New York. It proved to be an inspired choice. Stevie gave a brilliant, energetic performance and the audience went bananas. The atmosphere captured on the resulting album 'Recorded Live – the Twelve-Year-Old Genius' was electric and in marked contrast to his next live album, which was to appear seven years later. That was recorded at The Talk of the Town in London, where the West End night-club goers gave him a polite but restrained reception. He was hard put to it to make them sing along with even the title lines of one of his best-known hits.

In 1963 genius was a word that was already being blithely bandied around in connection with many artists, most of whom ill-deserved the title and soon faded from public memory, but even this early in his career Stevie had some just claim to such a title, if only on the strength of the number of instruments he played. His entry in the magazine the *Gramophone* described him as 'juvenile, teenbeat, bongos, drums, harmonica, organ, piano, vocal'.

The Apollo album was a bright, immediately likeable record, with Stevie managing to put life into even such dreary material as Ray Charles' 'Drownin' In My Own Tears'.

But the greatest achievement of that album was the two-part 'Fingertips'. It was in every sense a one-off. Nothing like it had been tried before and nothing like it ever happened again. Certainly it was far removed from anything else that has ever gone out stamped with Motown's label.

Stevie's exhilarating and distinctive harmonica solos were highly praised by the critics who could not then have known that this prodigious talent had first been nurtured on a four hole instrument that Stevie wore on a string round his neck. Everything seemed to go into those harmonica solos – even a snatch of a sailor's hornpipe!

'Everybody say yeah,' yelled Stevie, the brass responded and Clarence Paul came on and said Stevie was wonderful, as if they didn't already know. It was an exciting record, born out of the excitement of everyone who was there and all that remained to be seen was whether anyone would buy it. Either it would be a monster, it was

27

generally agreed at the record company, or else it would fail abysmally.

It was a monster. On June 22nd, 1963, a month and a day after its release, 'Fingertips' entered America's *Billboard* Hot 100 and climbed steadily to the number one position. In Britain, however, where it was Stevie's first British release, it did nothing.

The Apollo album was released on May 31st, by which time the title was already out of date since Stevie had turned thirteen. Still, twelve-year-old genius sounded better and he was actually twelve when the album was recorded, so, in a way, nobody was telling any lies.

Three more albums by Stevie appeared in the States in 1963, two of them released on the same date, July 16th. These both had self-explanatory titles – 'Tribute To Uncle Ray' and 'The Jazz Soul Of Little Stevie'.

'Tribute To Uncle Ray' was a collection of well-known Ray Charles numbers. Ray Charles was at the peak of his popularity in the early to mid-sixties and it was inevitable that comparisons should be made between him and the much younger Stevie, since both were black and blind, although Ray had not been blind since birth, but had sight which deteriorated rapidly in his childhood.

Much was made in the Press about Ray being Stevie's hero and some writers put it about that Ray was in fact Stevie's uncle, rumours which Motown took no great pains to deny.

Ray Charles, however, was not to sustain the momentum of his career. Ill-health and drug problems probably did little to help his work and the standard of his recordings became erratic. Today his reputation is founded largely on memories of his past work, although he is still a formidable talent. In recent years he has returned Stevie's tribute by recording some of his songs.

'Jazz Soul' was mainly a showcase for Stevie's drumming and is little remembered these days.

The fourth Stevie Wonder album to appear in 1963 was With A Song In My Heart', which might be dubbed the happy' album, containing as it does such songs as 'Make Someone Happy', 'Smile', 'Get Happy', 'On The Sunny Side Of The Street' and 'Put On A Happy Face'. This was a middle-of-the-road styled album all the way and the beginning of Motown's policy of getting Stevie to do anything that happened to be in vogue at the time. This policy continued with Stevie's only '64 album release, 'Stevie At The Beach'.

Stevie's early albums were all released in Britain as well as America, as were his singles from 'Fingertips' onwards.

'Fingertips' was followed by 'Workout Stevie Workout', an embarrassing attempt to harness his wildest excesses. Then came 'Castles In The Sand', taken from the 'Stevie At The Beach' album, and 'Hey Harmonica Man' in May 1964, when he ceased to be 'little'. 'Hey Harmonica Man' was only marginally more successful artistically than 'Workout Stevie Workout'. Stevie vocally was coming on like a Junior James Brown, but he was working with a conventional backing arrangement and singer and band scarcely fitted where they touched.

Stevie's late '64 – early '65 singles, 'Happy Street', 'Kiss Me Baby' and 'High Heel Sneakers', failed to bring him anything like the sales of 'Fingertips' and he had still to make an impression in Britain although his songs were getting airplay.

With 'Fingertips' he had established himself primarily as a live artist and he played many concerts to back up the reputation that the record had earned him. Some of the magic of the Apollo was happening in subsequent concerts all over America, although it was always hard to find places where a boy of his age would be allowed to play. In Britain, however, it was a different story.

His first UK visit was at Christmas 1963, when he flew over for promotional appearances on ITV's principal pop shows *Ready Steady Go* and *Thank Your Lucky Stars*. These failed to earn him a hit, but in the spring of the following year he was back to tour with the Motortown Review. The Motortown Review was headed by Martha and the Vandellas and the Miracles, with Georgie Fame and his group The Blue Flames appearing as special guests.

The tour must have been a depressing experience. Ticket sales were not good and the applause reaching Stevie from large half-empty auditoriums must have seemed hollow with his US triumphs still fresh in his memory. On that tour he came and went without conquering and it was to be nearly two years more before Britain finally succumbed to Stevie's seventh UK single release, 'Uptight'.

CHAPTER FOUR

When Stevie Wonder joined Motown, the company was still in its infancy, but within a few years it had gained a hugely impressive roster of artists including Marvin Gaye, Diana Ross and the Supremes, The Four Tops, The Temptations, Smokey Robinson, The Miracles, Gladys Knight and the Pips, Tammi Terrell, Mary Wells, Martha and the Vandellas, and, of course, Stevie.

Acres of press coverage have appeared on Motown artists over the years, but the workings of the company itself are still little known, simply because Motown is extremely secretive about itself. It used to be the only record company which would not submit to external audit so that sales figures could be verified for the collection of gold discs.

In the early days there was a good reason why the company did not welcome investigation into its business affairs for, although Motown was scrupulously honest in its treatment of its artists, it did not pay them very well. When Stevie picked up the money from his trust fund at the age of twenty-one, there was one million dollars in it (about £400,000 at the prevailing rates of exchange) and that was his reward for sales of almost 30 million records.

Motown, run by Berry Gordy and his family, acted as a parent for all its artists. It controlled everything from their stage routines to their bookings to the copyright of their songs. Many of the artists were from humble backgrounds and knew nothing about the handling of finance or of legal matters. Unlike most white performers they had no lawyers to negotiate their contracts and the accepted their royalty rates without question.

It might seem that Gordy was ripping his artists off, but it must be remembered that he was trying to make a success of a young company and that many of his artists including Stevie, went on later to secure extremely lucrative new deals with the company. But in the early sixties black recording stars tended not to make anywhere near as much money as their white counterparts.

Throughout Stevie's teenage years, Motown had extensive artistic as well as administrative control over his career. They did not have complete artistic control, because Stevie was writing a good deal of his own material but he knew what kind of material the company expected from him and that was what he provided.

Soon after he turned twenty-one and secured his new deal, he said, 'I have spent a lot of years pleasing other people. Now I'm going to please myself.' In his late teens he certainly felt that Motown was restricting his musical development, and was dismayed at being asked to jump through whatever musical hoops the company dictated.

The first album 'Recorded Live – The Twelve-Year-Old Genius' was a true picture of Stevie at that age, showing off his talents as well as revealing some of the excesses of his immaturity.

'Tribute To Uncle Ray' was a good PR exercise. By linking Stevie's name with that of Ray Charles, the company were increasing his chances of press coverage and Motown knew that the versions of the songs on the album stood up well to comparison with those by Charles himself. It was a mature album, even though the lyrics of

ome of the songs were quite unsuitable for a thirteen-
ear-old.

'The Jazz Soul Of Little Stevie' was simply an attempt
o point out Stevie's instrumental versatility, which it did
ery well, even though the pseudo-hip titles of some of
he tracks caused one or two critics to wince – titles like
Session No 112'.

After the first three albums, Motown decided that the
ime had come to lay off the more raw side of Stevie's
music and set him to singing more sophisticated, middle-
of-the-road material. Motown artists were groomed to play
swanky nightclubs, where the money was good. Stevie
might be too young to be allowed by the law to play
nightclubs yet, but if he were headed in the right direction early, he would be ready for those expensive venues
when the time came.

Stevie's fourth album 'With A Song In My Heart' was
full of songs familiar to every nightclub-goer – 'Smile',
'On The Sunny Side Of The Street' and so on.

Six months later, Stevie's fifth album showed that he
was off on another track. 'Stevie At The Beach' was a
collection of seaside songs, though not as much of a surf
party as the title might lead one to think. Alongside
material like 'Beachstomp' and the single 'Hey Harmonica Man' were more sophisticated songs such as 'Red
Sails In The Sunset', 'Ebbtide' and the haunting 'Sad
Boy', was another of those songs that had a lyric far too
adult for a singer of Stevie's age.

> When she reads in the paper
> that the sad, sad boy has drowned,
> will she laugh with him
> and say 'that funny clown'

On 'Sad Boy' Stevie's breathing was all over the place,

but he was later to turn breathlessness into an asset, usin
it deliberately for effect.

There was a gap of two years between the release o
'Stevie At The Beach' and his next album 'Uptight', fo
which schooling and his voice breaking were probabl
equally responsible. 'Uptight' was a landmark album i
several ways. It contained, in the title track, Stevie's firs
major contribution as a composer. Three hit singles wer
culled from the album in the States and 'Uptight' gav
Stevie his first big hit in Europe.

The album also showed how Motown could successfull
get one of their artists to assimilate everything else tha
was going on in the music scene and come out with
good, individual record.

'Uptight' was the obvious track to choose for a firs
single from the album, and when it succeeded, it was al
most inevitable that its successor would be 'Nothing Too
Good For My Baby', which was more of the same thing
In America it was a hit, but British buyers sensed that
despite being a great performance, it was virtually 'Up
tight' part two and left it alone.

The third single from the 'Uptight' album was al
together different, being a highly innovative version o
Bob Dylan's anthem 'Blowing In The Wind'. Stevie was
influenced by Dylan at the time and claimed, 'The
country feeling on "Uptight" comes from Dylan.'

Many artists, both black and white, have seen the disco
potential in Dylan's songs and capitalised on it with
varying degrees of success, but Stevie was one of the first.
His version of the civil rights song, on which he is joined
by Levi Stubbs, is all the more poignant for knowing that
both singers are black.

Elsewhere on the album, Stevie was experimenting with
his writing. Some things were rather too obviously bor-

34

owed. 'Pretty Little Angel', for example, might have been written by Neil Sedaka, whom Stevie admired. On other tracks one can see, in retrospect, that Stevie's sense of melody was only just beginning to develop. Too many of them are simply workings and elaborations on riffs rather than sustained tunes.

The 'Uptight' album was followed six months later by 'Down To Earth', another mixture of Wonder compositions and well-known songs by other people. It housed another Dylan song, 'Hey Mr Tambourine Man', which worked less well for Stevie than 'Blowin' In The Wind' had. Maybe he knew it; anyway, the song was not chosen as a single. Stevie's vocal was altogether too contrived and by chopping up the song lyrically he lost all sense of the words.

The major achievement of 'Down To Earth' was the single taken from it 'A Place In The Sun'. Stevie was to become a pastmaster at taking romantic ballads and turning them brilliantly into elegant disco smoochers. 'A Place In The Sun' was his first attempt at making this kind of transformation. It was an optimistic, likeable song written by Ron Miller and Bryan Wells and Stevie performed it with great maturity of style, despite being still only fifteen. The brief use of harmonica on this track shows commendable restraint and perfect taste.

After the two pot-pourri albums 'Uptight' and 'Down To Earth' Motown wanted something different, and the next album, 'I Was Made To Love Her', had Stevie whacking through eight R&B hits associated with other people, including 'Can I Get A Witness', 'Respect' and 'My Girl'. The best of them was Sam Cooke's 'Send Me Some Lovin' ', although the pace is a little too sluggish to be perfect.

The album itself was scarcely sensational, but the title

track single attracted rave reviews. David Morse, writing in his 1971 book *Motown*, described it as Stevie's 'best record to date', while *Rolling Stone*'s Jon Landau held that it 'transformed Motown and became art'. The song has been covered many times in all kinds of ways, ranging from a close harmony rendering by the Beach Boys to a clever tenor sax version by King Curtis.

Stevie's phrasing on his own version is delightfully imaginative. He shuns the precision of other Motown artists like the Supremes and goes for rough excitement in its place. Sometimes he lets himself lag behind the beat before racing to catch up. He also uses his breathless techniques to add momentum to the music. His superb performance earned him his third gold disc (the first two being 'Fingertips' and 'Uptight').

By this time, Stevie had enough successes behind him to warrant a greatest hits album and the one that emerged was good value for money, containing, as it did, sixteen tracks. The only sorry factor was the inane sleeve notes by one Scott Regan, who wrote: 'Steve talks about his blindness freely and considers it a gift from God' – piffle!

Around this time, Motown dreamed up the notion of a Stevie Wonder Christmas album and a very odd kettle of fish it turned out to be, encompassing everything from Marvin Gaye's hefty 'What Christmas Means To Me' to the nursery rhyme styled 'Bedtime For Toys' to Schubert's 'Ave Maria' and an idiotic piece of nonsense called 'One Little Christmas Tree', written by Ron Miller and Bryan Wells, who had been delighted with the success of Stevie's version of their 'A Place In The Sun'.

The one really interesting feature of the album was the title track 'Someday At Christmas', which was unique for Motown at the time. It contained the lines:

Someday at Christmas men won't be boys
Playing with bombs like kids play with toys

but was recorded long before the label handled political material and at a time when it was very much pro the American involvement in the Vietnam war.

The album 'Someday At Christmas' even took in such gems as the archly twee 'Little Drummer Boy' and curdlingly coy 'Twinkle Twinkle Little Me'. At Christmas, apparently, even the most hard-bitten of record company moguls go soft in the heart and soppy in the head and allow recordings to escape on to an unsuspecting public which grasp every maudlin sentiment that can be wrung out of the poor unfortunate festival.

After 'Someday At Christmas', Stevie exonerated Ron Miller from any blame attaching to the slushy 'One Little Christmas Tree' by reviving one of his best songs, 'For Once In My Life', which blossomed exquisitely out of an opening guitar figure. Russell Gersten, writing in *Rolling Stone*, said, 'The arrangement in general and Stevie's phrasing in particular, are brilliant.'

'For Once In My Life' earned Stevie his fourth gold disc, hitting number two in the American *Billboard* chart and number three in Britain. Curiously, the massive selling title track of the 'For Once In My Life' album was not the first single released from it, but the third. First came the indifferent 'Shoo-Be-Doo-Be-Doo-Da-Day'. Its catchy title line and infectious dance beat ensured its success, but it was a flimsy piece of material and possibly the weakest track on the whole album.

'You Met Your Match', the second single release from the album, was much better, boasting a good lyric about the battle of the sexes and featuring some exciting interplay between Stevie and his back-up singers.

The 'For Once In My Life' album is still rated as being one of Stevie's best. He wrote or co-wrote much of the material for it and gave assured performances on every track. On other people's songs, he gave a particularly good rendering of Bobby Hebb's 'Sunny' and even the most avid Billie Holliday fan could not complain that he had committed sacrilege with his moving version of her 'God Bless This Child'.

Motown had by now put Stevie through just about every conceivable musical style and began to make half-hearted moves to turn him into an all-round entertainer. He appeared on television doing comedy routines with American comic Flip Wilson and made guest appearances in two beach movies. In 'Muscle Beach Party' he appeared with the Supremes and in 'Bikini Beach' he was with the bald-headed Pyramids.

'Bikini Beach' was something of a misnomer, since Annette Funicello, who was booked to star in virtually every beach movie ever made, thought bikinis were indecent and flatly refused to be filmed in anything but a one-piece!

In the early years of Stevie's career, Motown had great difficulty in booking any television work for Stevie at all in America. Blind people tend to be exaggerated in their movements and television producers thought that the way Stevie jerked his head around might upset viewers. In Britain they were not so squeamish.

In the same month that the 'For Once In My Life' album came out in America, another Stevie Wonder album appeared, but only on the American market. It was called 'Alfie' and emerged on the Gordy label under the name Eivets Rednow (Stevie Wonder spelt backwards).

Most people figured out that this instrumental album

was by Stevie particularly as he sometimes played the title track in concert, but some people were taken in. Stevie remembers one black teenager saying to him, 'Man, these whites are takin' over everything. I heard a kid today, man, played "Alfie" just like you.'

'Oh yeah,' replied Stevie, kidding him along, 'You mean this cat Rednow? Well, don't you worry about him!'

In 1969 Stevie put out only one album, the unremarkable 'My Cherie Amour'. The only really worthy tracks on it were the two singles, the title song and 'Yester-Me, Yester-You, Yesterday'.

'My Cherie Amour' was a lovely song, containing one of Stevie's best ever melody lines, but Motown slipped up in not realising its potential straight away. It went out first as a B-side before being issued as an A-side.

The two singles were big hits both sides of the Atlantic, 'Yester-Me, Yester-You, Yesterday' earning Stevie his highest chart placing ever – number one in some charts, number two in others.

The main faults of the 'My Cherie Amour' album were first that its instrumentation was dull, and second that it did not seem to know whether it was going for the middle-of-the-road or disco market. Hence it included ballads like his own showbizzy composition 'Give Your Love' and disco numbers like a rave-up version of 'Hello Young Lovers'.

In the course of 1969 Stevie played an eighteen-date spring tour of Britain, and soon after his return home he went to the White House to pick up an award from President Nixon. The award was somewhat cumbersomely titled 'The President's Committee on Employment of Handicapped People's Award Distinguished Service Award.'

What Stevie thought of Nixon at the time is not recorded, but five years later he was to show absolute contempt for the man on his single 'He's Misstra Know-It-All'.

1969 was a landmark year for Stevie as far as Britain was concerned. His tour was an enormous success, he had his number one hit single, and, oddly, the below standard 'My Cherie Amour' album was his first to make the charts in the UK.

Britain was rewarded for its interest with its own live Stevie Wonder Album, one of the two in-concert LPs brought out in the course of 1970. The first was 'Stevie Wonder Live', released on both sides of the Atlantic and recorded at an unspecified American venue, and the second was 'Stevie Wonder Live At The Talk Of The Town', released only in the UK.

Both albums were much more restrained affairs than 'Fingertips', recorded seven years earlier, but of the two, the British one is generally regarded as the better.

The American 'Live' album was good value for money in terms of playing time, taking in seventeen cuts, but the stage performance misses out on the excitement of Stevie's studio work. The Motown sound is undeniably difficult to capture in concert, but the album offers no compensating virtues in the form of witty introductions or improvisations.

To British listeners the most important track is 'Alfie', since the studio recording of it was never issued in Britain either on album or as a single.

The other outstanding track on 'Live' is 'By The Time I Get To Phoenix' which features a barnstorming finish, in contrast to the interminable fadeouts of Stevie's studio recordings.

The rather lack-lustre performance on 'Live' was not

helped by the mixing, which was badly balanced and allowed an over-enthusiastic drummer to all but drown out Stevie's clarinet solo on 'Shoo-Be-Boo-De-Doo-Da-Day'.

The London live album was shorter, having only ten tracks, and six of the songs on it also figured on the American LP. Nevertheless it was a much worthier recording.

The album was intended to publicise the fact that Stevie had actually played The Talk Of The Town, one of the world's swankiest venues, but it was a fine work for all that. The audience could have been more voluble in their response, but Stevie was in fine form the night of the recording and the oft-criticised house band, augmented by Stevie's own musicians, did themselves proud.

One wonders what the audience in general made of remarks from Stevie like, 'If you don't be cool, I'll hit you so hard your socks'll roll up and down like windowshades,' or what Diana Ross, who was among the diners, thought of being told by him how good she looked! At any rate she did not join him onstage for a duet.

One person who was impressed by the recordings was Eric Clapton, who rated Stevie's version of Simon and Garfunkel's 'Bridge Over Troubled Water' enough to include it in his top ten list of favourite recordings.

'He slows it right down,' Eric explained. 'The dynamics are very heavy. It builds up and comes down to almost silence.' The treatment is certainly very effective. Stevie's voice at one point is backed only by the bass of Michael Henderson, who later went to play for jazzman Miles Davis.

Stevie's next studio album was released in August 1970 in America, with UK release following in December. It was called 'Signed, Sealed, Delivered' and was heralded as the first set of recordings Stevie had produced himself, which, as he explained, was not strictly true.

'I produced quite a lot of things before "Signed, Sealed", but they never got released.'

Stevie says simply, ' "Signed, Sealed" was the biggest thing I'd had up to that time.' It more than made up for the disappointment of 'My Cherie Amour'.

Talking to Phil Symes of *Disc and Music Echo* in 1971, Stevie said, 'It's only recently that I've started taking my career seriously – since I wrote "My Cherie Amour". I suddenly realised it was time I calmed down and started behaving responsibly.'

This new attitude shines through on 'Signed, Sealed, Delivered'. There is not one filler among the tracks, not a weak line anywhere and the album is still looked back on as the culmination of Stevie's career as a soul singer. It was a rough, tough album and as soulful as anything that had ever come out of Motown.

The outstanding track on the album was the mammoth hit single, 'Signed, Sealed, Delivered (I'm Yours)', which Stevie co-wrote with Syreeta Wright. Syreeta had been a Motown back-up singer who had worked with Stevie on his 'Live At The Talk Of The Town' album.

Syreeta explained to British-based American journalist Robin Katz how the collaboration came about.

'I read him my poetry and he put it to music just to show me that it could be done. The first time he tried, it was a song that ended up "Signed, Sealed, Delivered (I'm Yours)". When that sold two million copies, it really did convince me.'

'Signed, Sealed, Delivered (I'm Yours)' was a magnificent single, carved in the same mould as 'Yester-Me, Yester-You, Yesterday', but the whole thing only contained eight lines of lyric and they nearly ranked as poetry:

Ooo-ee, babe, you set my soul on fire,
That's why I know you're my one and only desire.

Apart from Syreeta, Stevie's mother, Lulu Hardaway and Lee Garrett also got in on the composing credits. With a song that simple in construction, it's hard to imagine what the hell they all found to contribute!

Lee Garrett was the first black artist signed to Chrysalis Records and, in their press release on him, the company made much of the fact that Lee had worked with Stevie Wonder. Lee had known Steve ever since his 'little' days and remembered, 'They used to put Stevie to bed at night and I'd go and wake him up and get him out of bed : the two of us would go out cruising around the town at 4 am.' So much for the eight hours sound sleep Stevie was supposed to be getting at that age!

'Signed, Sealed, Delivered (I'm Yours)' may have been the colossus of the album, but it was only the second of four singles to be released from it. The first was Stevie's own heart-rending ballad 'Never Had A Dream Come True' on which the interpretive powers of his voice were beautifully used. The song was later covered by another Motown artist Tata Vega, but she sounded as if she really had to work for the effects that came almost casually to Stevie.

The third single from 'Signed, Sealed' was a Ron Miller composition, an articulate plea against social injustice entitled 'Heaven Help Us All'.

The last single milked from the album was Stevie's version of the Beatles' 'We Can Work It Out', which has its admirers but does not work as well as the original. A lot of the appeal of the Beatles' version was attained by contrasting McCartney's sweetly pretty handling of the main theme with John Lennon's cryptic mid-section and

43

Stevie, with only one voice, could not hope to compete on those terms. Nevertheless, although his reading of the song was less cutting than the original, it made a feast of its rhythms and is reckoned by many to be the best treatment of a Beatles' number ever to come out of Motown.

All four singles were big hits. In Britain's *Music Week* charts 'Never Had A Dream Come True' reached number six, 'Signed, Sealed, Delivered (I'm Yours)' number fifteen, 'Heaven Help Us All' number twenty-nine, and 'We Can Work It Out' number twenty-seven. 'Signed, Sealed' and 'Heaven Help Us' collected gold discs for their maker.

In 1970 Stevie was presented with a Showbusiness Inspiration Award by 'Fight For Sight', an organisation promoting research into eye diseases. At about this time, Stevie began to explain to journalists his theory on the cause of his own blindness. He was born a month premature and was placed in an incubator. He believed that his blindness was caused by an insufficient supply of oxygen to the incubator, although blindness is always a possible consequence of babies being born premature and undersized.

By 1970 it was legally possible for Stevie to play American nightclubs and in March of that year he played his first headlining concert at the famous New York Copacabana nightclub.

During the course of 1970 Stevie moved out of the family home and found himself a place in New York and, on September 14th, he married Syreeta Wright. The couple told the world that they intended to have 'many babies'.

CHAPTER FIVE

Stevie Wonder's first contract with Motown, signed when he was eleven, lasted five years, and when its term was up, he readily signed up for a second five-year period. When 'Signed, Sealed, Delivered' came out, Stevie was in the final year of his second contract and thoroughly discontented with Motown. For ten years he had delivered everything expected of him and he was fed up with it. He felt that Motown's way of doing things was limiting his scope and cramping his development as an artist. He began to rebel.

After 'Signed, Sealed' he began to take in tracks to Motown that he knew were not in accordance with their formula and, naturally enough, the response was stony.

'I would get the product there,' he said, 'and nobody would listen to it and I'd say forget it, so a lot of things were left somewhat un-followed-up by me.' He felt as if he were still being treated by the company as 'Little Stevie Wonder', even though he was a six-foot-tall married man with ten years experience in the record business behind him.

Having left the family home, he was in an independent frame of mind and in the last year of his contract he could not wait to find out what Motown had been doing with his earnings as a minor. He became temporarily suspicious and truculent (uncharacteristic of a Taurean) and the album he delivered to his record company in

45

early 1971 was not at all the kind of LP they wanted from him. It was also a mistake, too much new ground broken too soon. He sensed that he had Motown over a barrel with his contract coming up for renewal, sensed freedom and was over-indulgent with it. He let it run away with him before he was ready to walk.

'Where I'm Coming From' was all wrong, but it did serve the purpose of giving Motown a very clear warning; let me do it my way – or else!

The critics did not know what to make of the album and it was roundly slated in most quarters. It did not help that Marvin Gaye was also making his big transition at the time with his 'What's Going On' and doing so far more smoothly and successfully.

In comparison with Marvin's change, Stevie's jump looked all the more gauche and self-indulgent.

Tamla's distress with their prodigal son was obvious. They had not got the slightest clue even how to package this new disc and may be pardoned for the aberration that was the cover for it. On the front of the sleeve were six large letters WONDER filled with pictures of Stevie, which you could press out and, with the aid of a string, make into a 'Wondermobile'. Two of the photographs on that sleeve showed Stevie in combat uniform, highly appropriate when one imagines what relations between Stevie and his label must have been like at the time!

The back of the sleeve was even worse. For the first time ever, a Motown album sleeve carried printed lyrics and they were not good, containing such lines as:

> *Sweet fragrance irritates*
> *In a stale room death awaits*
> *Persecute your own self-pride.*

They were maudlin, pretentious and had mostly been

written by Syreeta. It was all good fuel for the argument, first voiced by Mick Jagger, that musicians shouldn't take their wives (he called them old ladies) to the office.

Mercifully, it was not possible to put all the blame on Syreeta. Stevie, feeling that he was no longer tied to working within the frame of a three-minute single, ran amok with the studio tricks. The result was jumbled, embarrassingly overblown and detracted totally from the still unerring clarity of the vocals.

Vince Aletti wrote in *Rolling Stone*, more in sadness than anger, 'Already one of the most inventive, expressive singers performing today, Stevie apparently wanted an opportunity to loosen up outside the confines of a typical Motown single. But he blew it. Not only are the lyrics undistinguished, but much of the production and arrangement is self-indulgent and cluttered with effects that too often obscure the utter virtuosity of Wonder's singing.'

Stevie was later to admit the album's faults to one of Aletti's colleagues on *Rolling Stone*, Ben Fong-Torres.

' "Where I'm Coming From" was kinda premature to some extent, but I wanted to express myself. A lot of it now I'd probably remix. But "Never Dreamed You'd Leave In Summer" came from that album and "If You Really Love Me" ... but it's nothing like the things I write now (1973).'

'Never Dreamed You'd Leave In Summer' and 'If You Really Love Me' were, without doubt, the album's saving graces. The former was exquisitely covered by Joan Baez in '75 for her comeback LP, 'Diamonds And Rust', as well as being excellently handled by Three Dog Night. Both songs were issued as singles and fared well in the States, although only 'If You Really Love Me' made it in Britain, reaching number twenty in the *Music Week* chart.

Motown were obviously unhappy with 'Where I'm

Coming From', especially as, in sales terms, it was little short of a disaster, but they did not blow their top over it and left Stevie to make the first move afterwards. That he was only too ready to do.

Ewart Ebner, president of Motown, recalls, 'He came to me and said, "I'm twenty-one now, I'm not gonna do what you say any more. Void my contract." I freaked.' It's not surprising. The situation was very delicate and what happened within the next five minutes was crucial to whether Motown's biggest money spinner flew the nest or not. He did not. Abner must have done some pretty good soft-talking, but even so Stevie was not entirely convinced of the company's good intentions. When the time came to collect his childhood earnings, he had the administration of them vetted through the courts where it was found that everything had been totally above board.

Stevie relented. Despite enticing offers from other companies, he decided to stay with Motown, although he kept them hanging on for six months before he made his mind up, and the deal that was finally concluded was far removed from the kind of contracts Motown were accustomed to making with their artists.

The new arrangement, negotiated by Johannan Vigoda, Stevie's lawyer and the man who acted as attorney for Jimi Hendrix and Ritchie Havens among others, was a great wad of a document, running to one hundred and twenty pages. It secured for Stevie his own publishing, a thing unthinkable at Motown beforehand, and a generous royalty rate.

Stevie has never actually said what that rate was, although he stated that it made him secure, but one close associate has guessed, probably accurately, that it was fifty per cent.

Vigoda knew that the contract he was negotiating with

48

Motown on behalf of one of its artists was of enormous significance.

'It was a very important contract for Motown,' he said, 'and a very important contract for Stevie, representing the artists of Motown. He broke tradition; he opened up the future for Motown. That's what they understood. They had never had an artist in thirteen years; they had singles records, they managed to create a name in certain areas, but they came through with a major, major artist. It turned out they did a beautiful job.'

At this time, apparently, even Marvin Gaye had not managed to secure a similar deal for himself.

Spencer Leigh of the British magazine *Blues and Soul* wrote, 'Until he came over, I'd thought that Marvin Gaye had a similar arrangement (to Stevie) and now I'm not sure whether he's been badly done or is just one of nature's complainers.'

Before the new deal was concluded, Motown, worried perhaps that they were going to get nothing more, pushed out a 'Greatest Hits Part Two' compilation, a good value buy containing: 'Shoo-Be-Doo-Be-Doo-Da-Day', 'Signed, Sealed, Delivered (I'm Yours)', 'If You Really Love Me', 'For Once In My Life', 'We Can Work It Out', 'You Met Your Match', 'Never Had A Dream Come True', 'Yester-Me, Yester-You, Yesterday', 'My Cherie Amour', 'Never Dreamed You'd Leave In The Summer', 'Travellin' Man' and 'Heaven Help Us All', the sentiment of the last track being shared by the whole company!

When Motown made the new deal with Stevie, they had amazing faith and vision, because on the face of it, he had just made one album they did not want at all and seemed hellbent on doing more of the same thing. All the same, he was not only valuable as a property in his own right as a recording artist. He had already proved himself as a successful producer of other people's records.

The first record he produced for anyone but himself was 'It's A Shame' for the Detroit Spinners. It was a massive hit and the only Spinners' record that made any notable impression on the British charts. He was deeply hurt that a second record that he produced for the Spinners, 'We'll Have It Made', failed to make it. He had also produced tracks for Martha Reeves and David Ruffin, although the results never reached the public. Nevertheless, his potential as a producer was clearly an extra weapon when it came to bargaining over his contract.

Before Stevie signed up for his third five years with Motown, he took time out for some heavy thinking. There was no question of him wanting to take Motown for a ride and he was dismayed by the failure of 'Where I'm Coming From', both commercially and artistically, as were his record company. But if he was resolved that the mistakes of that album must never happen again, he was equally convinced that he could not return to the safe haven of the Motown formula.

First of all, he just holed up in New York with his new bride and then began to work out what was needed to get his new direction right. He played around with sound systems in his flat, then flew west to attend classes in musical theory and composition at the University of Southern California.

He especially wanted to study the uses of the Moog and ARP synthesisers. These new-fangled gadgets had been used for some years on recordings, but were still regarded largely as novelties and gimmicks, okay for avant-garde freaks like Walter Carlos, but no go for anybody concerned with making commercially acceptable music. Walter Carlos, at this time, had still to produce his devastatingly effective score for the movie *A Clockwork Orange*.

It was not until the late sixties that synthesisers even acquired keyboards, so until then they were of no practical use to anybody and even then they began to be used only for spacey effects by people like The Pink Floyd and experimental fringe groups like Tangerine Dream. Why, even the Moody Blues made their first futuristic albums with nothing but a very straight orchestra.

Stevie was the first artist to realise that the synthesiser could cease being merely freaky, and play a valuable role in the making of acceptable mass-market music. He wanted to turn it into a dancing machine and use it to underline the emotions in his songs.

'The great thing about electronic music,' he enthused, 'is that you can make things larger than life. You can choose colours and you can make the sounds of an instrument that does not exist.'

In his quest to find a place for synthesisers in his music, Stevie owed a great debt to his programmers, Malcolm Cecil and Bob Margouleff. 'I just tell them the kind of things I want,' he said, 'and they do it.'

Margouleff and Cecil built their own mammoth synthesiser and named it Tonto. They then made an album, 'Tonto's Expanding Headband', which was interesting, if typical, synthesiser music, but have since gone on to work with many illustrious artists, adding new dimensions to all kinds of repertoires.

For his next album, 'Music Of My Mind', Stevie spent a great deal of his own money – about a quarter of a million dollars – on studio time learning everything he could about synthesisers. The new album was an enormous achievement because Stevie played virtually everything on it, as the sleeve notes explain.

'This album is virtually the work of one man. All of th
songs are composed, arranged and performed by Stevi
Wonder (with guitar solo by Buzzy Feiton on "Supe
woman" and a trombone solo by Art Baron on "Lov
Having You Around") on piano, drums, harmonica
organ, clavichord, clavinet and Arp and Moog Syn
thesisers.'

Unfortunately the rest of the sleeve notes go well ove
the top. First in verse:

> *Stevie Wonder comes of age*
> *in now time*
> *into his own.*
>
> *A genius youth grew up with*
> *sings a new song*
> *now he's free.*
>
> *The man is his own instrument.*
> *The instrument is an orchestra.*
>
> *Stevie draws his vision*
> *from the world of pure vibration,*
> *which is music, feeling, energy.*
> *He builds his world in sound.*
>
> *Sensitive and earthy*
> *he sings and plays,*
> *like a child with joyful spirit*
> *yet with a master's depth and skill.*

If those words were not enough, there is one final paragraph which is ridiculously reverent. 'This album marks
a milestone in the development of a great talent. A man
who keeps his promise, Stevie in maturity shines with that

same loving and brilliant light that has drawn people to him for a decade. Born a star, he never lets his technical and artistic proficiency overshadow his deep humility. This album is a gift to the spirit from one who really cares.' The writer chooses to be anonymous!

By way of compensation, the sleeve is, in all other aspects, admirable. The front and back feature half profile portraits of Stevie with other pictures of himself mirrored in the lenses of his glasses, while the centrefold contains all the lyrics and a colourful picture montage.

All the songs on the album are written or co-written by Stevie (one with his wife, Syreeta Wright, and two with Yvonne Wright – no relation). Production is by Stevie, with Moog wizards Margouleff and Cecil credited as 'Associate Producers, Engineering, Moog Programming'.

Penny Valentine of *Sounds*, talking to Stevie Wonder about 'Music Of My Mind', asked him how long this music had been inside him before he made his break with Motown.

'A long, long time,' he answered. 'I can't say exactly when. There have always been things I've wanted to do. I've always been like a year ahead of my records and my performances somehow. There was a time when I played clarinet on a tape and played that through speakers and sang along with it – out of the blue at a club I was doing and it flipped everybody out. That was about four years ago.'

He went on to say that he had not formulated exactly what he was going to do when he went in to cut 'Music Of My Mind'. 'Whatever was on that album was just that it felt good to me, it felt right. I'd done a lot of recording, a lot of things. When I put it together all those things felt right.'

He told Penny Valentine that he had had trouble

convincing people that he could write, produce and play everything himself. 'Nobody believed me, nobody. Everyone said, 'Oh c'mon, don't give me no bull." But basically I never worry about anything like that. I never worry too much about what a person thinks.

'Motown just didn't understand. It was a thing of them saying, "This is a winning formula – why do you wanna go and do this?" Which is what a lot of people feel. Like they say I should stick to my own kind of style like, "I ain't got nothin' against what you're doing, but cut that rubbish out." '

Once 'Music' was finished, Stevie felt very good, but in America sales of the album were disappointing and it took Stevie time to work out why. 'I think maybe it was because it didn't really have a fantastic single. It was more of an album than something you could easily take a single off. I didn't feel with "Music" that here was a good chance to give out with some craziness, I just felt that the doors were open for me to play.'

Although Stevie did not reckon that the album contained a 'fantastic single' two singles were released from it in the States – 'Superwoman' and 'Keep On Running', although only 'Superwoman' was released in Britain, and it failed to make the charts, even though the LP sold well here.

Worldwide the album may not have sold as well as Stevie had hoped it might, but the critics, almost without exception, went into raptures about it, and now Stevie felt the time had come to take his new music out to reach a much bigger audience than he had done before.

He was booked to support the Rolling Stones on a fifty-date American tour, stretching from Vancouver to New York. By doing so, he would reach an audience that was predominantly white and orientated in its tastes towards rock and roll rather than the Motown sound.

As Stevie told *Rolling Stone* magazine, 'It wasn't a money-making thing, that wasn't the idea – exposure was the thing.

'I want to reach the people. I feel there is so much through music that can be said, and there's so many people you can reach by listening to another kind of music besides what is considered to be your only kind of music. That's why I hate labels where they say, "This is Stevie Wonder and for the rest of his life he will sing 'Fingertips'" ... maybe because I'm a Taurean and people say that Taureans don't dig change too much. I say as long as it's change to widen your horizons, it's cool.'

The tour was a huge success both for Stevie and the Stones, but after it was all over there was a rather sordid bit of bad-mouthing of Stevie in the Press by Stones' guitarist Keith Richard. One magazine claimed that Richard had called Stevie names, because he pulled out of one gig on the tour. The reason given was that Stevie had no drummer for the concert, but apparently it got around that Stevie was partying when he should have been working.

When the *Rolling Stone* magazine gave Stevie a chance to put his side of the story, he said, 'If Keith did say that, he's just childish, because I love people too much to just want to screw up and miss a show. And it's crazy, the things he said, if they were said – and if he did not say them, he should clarify them, because I will always hold this against him; I can't really face him, I'd feel funny in his presence.

'I had mixed emotions about where he was comin' from, you know, so I wouldn't be surprised if he said it, but I'm not too surprised about anybody saying anything about anything. What really bugged me about the whole thing was that our drummer was in a bad situation, mentally and spiritually, and that's why he left. What climaxed the whole thing was, we got into an argument. I told him he was rushing the tape – this was in Fort Worth, Texas – and he said, "I tell you what: you know how to play the harmonica, you take the mike, you sing and play drums and all that at the same time, 'cause I quit," and he split. I called up the Stones and said, "Look, man, our drummer left, and we might not be able to make the gig, so we'll try to make the second one but we won't be able to make the first show." And they said, "OK, that'll be cool." The next thing, I saw the Stones and they heard the new drummer and said, "Oh, out of sight!" Then the next thing was I read all this.'

That was not the only ill-feeling directed at Stevie around that time. English guitarist Jeff Beck, with whom Stevie had been working, got angry because he claimed that Stevie had promised him his song 'Superstition' as a single, but then went and put it out as a single himself first.

Stevie's version was explained, once again, in *Rolling Stone*. 'Well, I'd written a thing for them (Jeff Beck's group) – they wanted "Maybe Your Baby", and I said, "No, do this, this is even better," and I wrote "Superstition" that same night. And they wanted the track, which I couldn't give them, 'cause of Motown, so I said, "I'll give a seven (a $7\frac{1}{2}$ ips tape) and you all work on it and I'll play on the session," 'cause he said he'd play on the thing of mine. And I wrote another thing for them which was even more like Jeff Beck, a thing called "Thelonius", which they haven't done anything with . . . but I told him I was using "Superstition" for my album. The tune I wanted to release as a single was "Big Brother", but that was done too late to come out as a single. Motown decided they anted to release "Superstition". I said Jeff wanted it and they told me I needed a strong single in order for the album to be successful. My understanding was that Jeff would be releasing "Superstition" long before I was going to finish my album: I was late giving them "Talking Book". Jeff recorded "Superstition" in July, so I thought it would be out. But I did promise him the song, and I'm sorry it happened and he came out with some of the arrogant statements he came out with.

'I was crazy that there was so much fuss over a single from "Talking Book", because the album was loaded with potential hit singles. Apart from "Superstition", which was of course, released as a single, there was "Big Brother", which wasn't, "You Are The Sunshine Of My Life", which was the follow-up to "Superstition", and at least two more possible contenders.'

Penny Valentine wrote in *Sounds* in 1973 that 'Music Of My Mind' and 'Talking Book' together represented the greatest thing that had happened to contemporary music since The Beatles' 'Sergeant Pepper', six years before. To this day 'Talking Books' remains my personal favourite of all Stevie's albums.

The album, like its predecessor, took a long time to record, longer than Stevie himself had anticipated, which was why it was late being delivered to Motown. The cover featured Stevie with a new corn crow hairstyle and, on the American copies, the title was printed both in ordinary print and braille. Some of the British copies were also produced with the braille title and one of them was presented to Stevie. He ran his fingers over it and looked puzzled.

'Why did they do that?' he asked. 'It says, "Picture Book"!'

'Talking Book' came out in Britain in January, 1973,

57

two months after its appearance in America, and i[n]
February Stevie was in London for promotional work, s[o]
journalists had plenty of opportunity to talk to him abou[t]
his new LP.

Many of the questions asked were about the politica[l]
nature of one of the songs, 'Big Brother' in particular an[d]
the album in general, on account of Stevie being dresse[d]
in long robes and beads for the cover shot.

Stevie explained the clothing to Tony Norman of th[e]
New Musical Express. 'I'm very black-orientated. I lov[e]
African clothes and stuff and I think it's beautiful the wa[y]
people are finding their own identity now. They are get[-]
ting over that thing of being ashamed of their heritage[.]
You can see it with hairstyles.

'At one time black people used to have their hair dye[d]
or straightened. Now they're proud of having their ow[n]
identity. It's very healthy.

'Some of the black movies may have helped things alon[g]
indirectly. "Shaft" probably did that more than "Super[-]
fly".'

Stevie admitted that his song 'Big Brother' had bee[n]
inspired by George Orwell. He told Penny Valentine: '[I]
saw the movie (of *1984*) on television but I didn't like i[t]
as much as the book – except the rats! Sure the idea wa[s]
from the book. I read it about six years ago – I used to b[e]
a very learned man until I turned into a musician and
majored seven chords back at thirteen. I feel that *1984* i[s]
pretty close to what's happening now, even though I don't
profess to know exactly what's going to happen in the
future.

'I don't think *1984* frightened me as much as it made
me think. Like the lines in the song "Your name is Big
Brother – you say that you're watching me on the telly",
that's about a certain kind of people. The people that

atch black people in the ghettos, watching people that
on't have too much. It's kinda force against force. Like
guerrilla warfare – like "I can't wait to see your face be-
ind my door" – that's the reaction it brings.'

It's interesting to note that Stevie said he 'saw' the
m *1984* on television. Even though he is blind, he is
ery fond of television and going to the movies and he
as no doubt able to imagine the rats just as well as most
eople could see them.

There were very few pursuits which Stevie allowed his
blindness to prevent him from following. In 1973 he even
oasted to *Rolling Stone* that he had once flown a plane.
It was a) Cessna or something, from Chicago to New
ork. Scared the hell out of everybody.'

'Who was your co-pilot?' asked the journalist. 'God?'

'No,' laughed Stevie. 'This pilot was there and he just
t me handle this one thing and I say, "What's this?"
nd we went whish, whoop.' Having flown a plane, he
aid his next ambition was to drive a car, something Ray
Charles had already done. He had driven one round an
irfield and nearly given his passenger a heart-attack.

People in talking to Stevie about his blindness have
sked him about his conception of colour, and he seems
o have got colours well sorted out in his mind. 'I have an
dea of what colours are. I associate them with the ideas
hat've been told to me about certain colours. I get a
ertain feeling in my head when a person says "red" or
blue", "green", "black", "white", "yellow", "orange",
purple" – purple is a crazy colour to me. Brown is a
ittle duller than green isn't it?'

Some people erroneously imagine that blind people
ee' black. They do not, they see nothing. The sense of
ight is completely missing.

By the time 'Talking Book' reached the public, Stevie

was well underway with his next album 'Innervision' which completes a trio of albums often grouped togeth in assessments of Stevie's work.

'Where I'm Coming From' is now thought of as rehearsal for Stevie's new music, which gelled so beau fully on his next album, 'Music Of My Mind', the first the trio.

On 'Music' a relaxed and assured Stevie allowed songs to range over a variety of themes, including on t album whatever, as he put it, 'felt right'.

'Talking Book' and 'Innervisions' were more precise their subject matter, the first dealing primarily with t love of man for woman, the second being concerned wi love of humanity in general.

Between them 'Talking Book' and 'Innervisions' mad Stevie the most highly rated contemporary artist in t world. In 1974, he was nominated for no less than sev Grammy Awards (the musical equivalent of the fil Oscars) and carried off five of them: Album of the Yea 'Innervisions'; Best Pop Performance – Male, 'You A The Sunshine Of My Life'; Best R&B Vocal Performan – Male, 'Superstition'; Best R&B Song, 'Superstition'; Be Engineered Non-Classical recording, 'Innervisions'.

The following year, Stevie was to collect a whole hea more Grammy Awards for his next album and in 1976, very relieved Paul Simon, after being presented with th Album Of The Year Award for his 'There Goes Rhymir Simon', thanked Stevie Wonder 'for not making an albur this year'!

'Innervisions' was another monumentally brillian work, full of tension and excitement and rich in potentia hit singles. Four of them were released: 'Higher Ground judged by many to be his best song ever; 'Living For Th City'; 'He's Misstra Know-It-All' (UK only) and 'Don'

You Worry 'Bout A Thing'.

When he had finished 'Innervisions', but before it was released, Stevie set out on a jazz and blues festival tour of America. Adam Block reported for the *New Musical Express* from one of the concerts, The Berkeley jazz and blues festival at Oakland stadium near San Francisco, and I make no apologies for quoting his review at length, since this was to be one of the last stage appearances Stevie would make for a long time.

'Now this monstrous structure [the stadium] holds about 70,000 baseball fans in the capacity it was designed for, and the promoters decided to rope off one half, drop the stage in the middle of the field a good half mile from the front bleachers, and set up a fan of four flanking video screens to provide the illusion of a live performance.

'They sold about 12,000 tickets to a crowd that was about eighty per cent Superfly, fashion flaunting black locals, and twenty per cent finger-popping dirt-balls and crab-ridden long-hair panhandlers.

'Now I think the promised groups appeared, but to be honest with you, the distant images on screen could have been a team of Chinese deep-knee-bend experts.

'How any collusion with an audience is supposed to cross a baseball field, and what relationship a windswept highpower amplification system has to musical fidelity or music itself, is a bit past me.' Conditions, you will have gathered, were far from ideal.

'The show began at eight o'clock. It was opened by The Heritage Hall Jazz Band, followed in succession by Esther Phillips, Rahsaan Roland Kirk and The Staple Singers.

'Stevie Wonder took the stage (after the Staples) past midnight as a cold wind was beginning to race over the stadium and the exasperation of being so far from the stage was beginning to make itself felt.

'Having nabbed the throne as King of Soul from both James Brown and Sly Stone, Wonder is one of the most respected and popular musicians on the planet these days

'He isn't a dangerous riot-inspiring superstar, but a real professional.

'Stevie opened the show with full band, and red, black and green satin-gowned ladies pumping behind, with "You've Got It Bad Girl" [from "Talking Book"], shifting from keyboard to drums, and back to ivories -- throwing in a harp solo that could have passed for a clarinet, in a loose jazzy version that upped the tempo a notch or two from the recorded version.

'Next he introduced a number entitled "Visions" from his upcoming album "Innovations" [Adam Block must have misheard the title announced through a distorting amplification system]. It's a rich glorious ball and Stevie's slant is on the "Imagine" concept.

'This led to "Think I'm On The Right Side". With letter perfect precision and no break, Stevie began a fast scat and headed up a double-time version of "I Was Made To Love Her", which broke into a wailing sax that traded with a nearby chanting rendering of the chorus.

'Stevie was moving like a pro, but perhaps a bit too much like a pro for this audience. There may be a certain "taking for granted" that comes with being so fine, and as he was cooling his way through "Golden Lady" [from "Innervisions"] with its stifled horns and climbing chorus, it was obvious that the audience was filing out in rather substantial numbers. After all, he hadn't really gotten them on their feet, and it was a chill evening.

'He turned to "My Cherie Amour" with only cymbal and horns punctuating his glissanding vocal, then cracked direct into another double-time, "Signed, Sealed, Deivered", and with a razzing sax lifting the sand, the folks began to shake a bit.

'A wah-wah guitar laced out the solo, horns grabbed the chorus in shattering climbing riffs, and the guitar led back to a long bluesy break as Stevie called, "Put Your Hands Together", signalling encouragement from the drums.

'As the band raved and the three ladies filed off stage, Stevie took to his vocal wah-wah tube and bent the song through bizarre, stretched and crowded tones, with only the bass behind him.

'He moved straight into the slow, beautiful, impeccable menthol-smooth hit "Sunshine Of My Life" and played through the applause to a rousing "Superstition", which had the remaining audience on their feet and moving.

'It was a fine, near faultless set in terms of pure music, but it never achieved the kind of contact the Staples had. Somehow the event itself took precedence in the minds of both Stevie and the promoters over any drive to ignite a relationship between the audience and performer.

'Wonder, if he was conscious of the situation, chose not to fight it.'

CHAPTER SIX

The Oakland Stadium concert was in early July, 1973. 'Innervisions' came out simultaneously in Britain and America on August 3rd. Three days after that Stevie Wonder lay in hospital close to death with multiple head injuries.

On August 6th, Stevie was travelling through South Carolina on his way from one concert to the next. He was making the journey along a two lane road between Greenville to Raleigh in a car, being driven by Stevie's cousin John Harris, and the vehicle had one other passenger, Stevie's drummer.

Harris was trying to pass a logging truck that was weaving from lane to lane in front of him, when the trucker suddenly slammed on his brakes and stopped abruptly. The logs from the truck slid off the back and crashed through the windscreen on Stevie's side of the car.

Stevie was sleeping at the time, sitting with his head slumped forward, his chin resting on his chest. If he had been awake and sitting upright, he would have been decapitated.

The three occupants of the car and the lorry driver were rushed to hospital in Salisbury, North Carolina, and were then transferred to an intensive care hospital in the nearby town of Winston for specialist treatment.

Stevie was in a coma for four days and a semi-coma for a further week. At first it seemed unlikely that he would survive, but then, when it became clear that he was not going to die, doctors' main fears were that he might have suffered extensive brain damage.

All the while he lay in a coma, Stevie's close friend and advisor Ira Tucker refused to leave his bedside and sang the words of 'Higher Ground' in his ear. The first sign they had that he would recover was when he moved his fingers as though at the keyboards and murmured along with the words Ira was singing.

Stevie regained consciousness to find that he had lost, at least temporarily, most of his sense of smell and he was worried that he might also have lost another faculty, the ability to play.

'When he came out of the coma,' Ira Tucker said later, 'we brought one of his instruments – I think it was the clarinet – to the hospital. For a while, Stevie just looked at it. Didn't do anything with it. You could see he was afraid to touch it, because he didn't know if he still had it in him – he didn't know if he could still play. And then when he did finally touch it! – man, you could just see the happiness spreading all over him. I'll never forget that.'

After he had recovered from the accident, Stevie told an American journalist, 'I would like to believe in reincarnation. I would like to believe that there is another life. I think that sometimes your consciousness can happen on this earth a second time around.

'I wrote "Higher Ground" before the accident, but something must have been telling me that something was going to happen to make me aware of a lot of things and to get myself together. This is like my second chance for life, to do something or to do more, and to value the fact that I am alive. And if I felt that not living would be better, to conclude it.'

Did you feel at any time that you had left your body? was another question.

'I did feel that way. I know that I probably did but I don't know where I went or ... because what happened to me was a very, very critical thing and I was really supposed to die.'

Stevie went on to say that he felt rushed to complete his work.

'I've always felt that way. It's not because of the accident. I'm not looking forward to being sixty or seventy, or even fifty. I'm just looking forward to being here as long as I can and will be. And the reason I may be doing a lot of things is because I feel that tomorrow is not promised to anyone; so it is important to me to do as much as I can today. I don't really think too much about tomorrow but I will do as much planning as I think is necessary. That's why if I never receive another Grammy or whatever, it's just the way life is. I have enjoyed what I have been given and I have received more than a lot of people.'

The car accident obviously meant that the second half of Stevie's jazz festival tour had to be cancelled, as did a big late summer concert scheduled for Stevie at London's White City.

Nobody could have guessed at the time of the accident how quickly Stevie would manage to be back. His first public appearance after the crash was only six weeks and a day from the date that it happened. To thunderous applause, he made a surprise appearance at Elton John's Madison Square Garden concert in New York on September 25th, where he jammed along with Britain's bespectacled superstar on 'Honky Tonk Women'.

Observers at the concert said that he still looked a little shaky and that his facial scars were worse than they had expected, but, in truth, it was a remarkable recovery.

The scars have now faded and mostly disappeared, but Stevie has suffered, since the accident, from occasional bad headaches, to which he was never prone before, and for the first two years after it happened he tended to tire easily, whereas beforehand everyone had envied his energy, which would keep him going through commitments that left everyone else flagging from exhaustion.

The accident has made a significant contribution to Stevie's work as a composer. As will be seen in discussion of his later albums, he has tended to continue to look ever more inward and become less worldly, more spiritual.

After his convalescence following the accident, Stevie began to hint at his possible eventual retirement. He said that he would be touring less. 'I'm fed up with always runnin' up and down the road,' was the way he put it, and would be spending more time in studio producing records both for himself and other people.

His output has certainly slowed down. Since the accident he has put out only two albums, albeit the second of them being a double album with an extended play record thrown in for free.

His concerts too have been more infrequent, although the standard of his performance has gone on reaching ever higher plains.

Stevie Wonder returned to performing full concerts less than six months after the car crash with a series of sell-out shows at London's Rainbow Theatre.

Andrew Tyler, of the *New Musical Express*, was present at the first two of these concerts and I quote his review in full, since it shows just how different two shows can be, even for an artist of Stevie's calibre. Perhaps some nervousness about his return in the full glare of publicity accounts for the disparity between the shows.

Tyler writes: 'His gold star friends all seem to have

67

booked seats for the second house with the noticeable exception of Ringo Starr, who can be observed in a black furry rug coat, and Bowie who, legend goes, called the box office with a request for a block of twenty seats and was told not to be so silly. So Bowie's not here.

'Anyway it's Stevie's night, and as he came hopping out with Wonder Love girl Shirley Brewer steering him from behind, he's greeted with hysterical screaming and whistling. He's making for Ollie Brown's drum kit and he's going to play a solo. It's a very long solo. A very long and boring solo that sets him off badly with the audience. Can he recover?

'His first genuine melody is the new instrumental "Contusion", a stirring piece of tempo playing – but Stevie's taking it too fast and confusing his rhythm section. The same observation can be made about "Higher Ground" and "You've Got It Bad Girl". He's so obviously unsettled he can't seem to come together with his band or his audience.

'It's going incredibly wrong: "Keep On Running", "Mary Ann" (a new one) and "Living For The City" scoot all over the place and by the time he reaches his greatest song "All In Love Is Fair", he's throwing off intros of half a dozen songs, cutting them dead, and then starting on something else.

'The best moments come with "Sunshine Of My Life" and "Superstition", which lead you to believe that if he gets it together for the second house it could still be a remarkable evening.

'But the band look distressed. The girls look distressed and Stevie is not enjoying his first concert since the accident. He leaves the stage with his ARP cracking out sten-gun noises and an audience more disappointed for Stevie than themselves.'

Tyler then moves on to describe the second house.

'The biggies have all shown up.

'The Staples, Paul and Linda Macca [McCartney], Clapton, Blue Mink, Linda Lewis, Diddy David Hamilton and the man from *Man About The House* [Richard O'Sullivan]. Who else? Townshend, Denny Laine, Jimmy McCulloch, Kiki Dee...

'It already feels more important and with the introduction that lists his achievements over the past seven months (two gold albums, three gold singles) you sense it can't be as bad as the opener.

'The drum solo is out. Instead he moves straight for his keyboards and slides into a much stronger version of "Contusion", a phenomenal delivery of "Higher Ground" and "You've Got It Bad Girl". I doubt if it's possible for two shows to be more unalike. It's all a question of attitude.

'The Wonderman is giving his band a chance to hook into his slipstream, instead of shaking them up so badly that the whole thing curdles. Not that they have a clue what he's going to do next and, even when they do, there's a good chance he's changed his mind. But they're with him. The audience is with him and everything is wonderful.

'Some oldies like "Signed, Sealed And Delivered" and "Uptight", a slack version of "Living For The City" and then a ridiculously insane Spanish rap to introduce "Don't You Worry 'Bout A Thing", And this time he plays "All In Love Is Fair" the decent way. No cracks, no pausing in mid-line.

'For a new number called "Twas A Sky-Blue Afternoon" he draws up a couple from the audience and gets them to hang around him. Rudeness. His rapport with the audience is astonishing and they don't just like him because he can't see. Enough, enough.

'This time he ends on a drum solo. It's a good one.

'AFTERMATH. I remember Ringo saying he wished he could sing like Stevie Wonder and I remember Clapton saying that Wonder is the best drummer in the world.

'There are several hundred people backstage drinking scotch and slapping members of the band on the back. There goes Eric Clapton, appearing plump and well and looking like he's got an MG Midget parked round the front with the hood down.

'And there's Stevie still sitting between friends on the sofa ...'

Tyler was not the only one to be that impressed with the second Rainbow show. Bryan Southall, at one time Motown's press officer in London, told me only recently, 'That show has to be one of the three best concerts I've seen by anyone anywhere. And I've never heard one voice sound so strong. If the microphone had packed up on him, he could have carried on just as well without it.'

Melody Maker's Geoff Brown described the show in one word, 'Magnificent.'

It seems likely that Stevie allowed himself to get over-tense before the first Rainbow show. At any rate, before it he was complaining volubly in his hotel room. When he asked to go over to the Rainbow early before the show to allow plenty of time for final rehearsal and sound-checking, he was told that was not possible as a photocall had been set up and he could not very well miss it.

'I'm a little upset,' Stevie replied, 'about what we've been doing and not been doing these past few days. We've been moving around so much we ain't really had time to get down to rehearsals.

'This is an important show and I want things to be right. There's gonna be a lot of people and critics out there and it's not that I'm scared but I just wannit to be right.' As it turned out, he had to content himself with it being right second time round.

Even though he was a little worried about how much the demands of the Press were eating into his rehearsal time, he was polite and jaunty towards all-comers and there were plenty of them. Nearly every journalist who went to see him in his hotel suite remarked that the place looked as if a bomb had hit it. There was a debris of Stevie's instruments everywhere, interminable half-finished glasses of lukewarm champagne, provided for the visitors, and a ridiculous number of people all trying to get their stories together. Stevie would find himself, completely disorientated, trying to say hello to twelve different voices at once, firing questions from all around him.

Nevertheless, he managed to keep them all amused. He did impersonations, Cary Grant being generally reckoned his best, told a joke about how only blind men put notes of different denominations in separate pockets so they know which ones to take out and pay taxis with, and made a play for the only girl among the assembled throng.

He had not known she was there until she asked when he would be making his next album.

'When I feel right,' he answered vaguely.

'And what makes you feel right?' she persisted.

'You do,' he responded, flashing her a broad grin.

One of Stevie's favourite tricks during interviews was to bring out his cassette player and play new songs he had recorded to journalists, who, convinced they had been given an exclusive preview of something from his next album, would dash back to their offices and write reams about his next move. More often than not they were disappointed as the song they had heard never reached the public.

By the time he came to London for those first important post-accident concerts, Stevie was already shaping up his next album, which was to be released in July later that year.

'Fullfillingness' First Finale' was to be his most written-about album ever, particularly as critics sensed in the title that Stevie might be heading for retirement. If there were not going to be many more Stevie Wonder recordings, then they had better make the most of what did come out seemed to be the general feeling.

Just before 'Fullfillingness' was due to appear, Stevie was in a studio in Los Angeles waiting to produce a single for Michael Jackson. But Michael had a bad throat and failed to show up, so somebody decided to treat the studio visitors to an airing of Stevie's newly completed work instead.

'I think,' said Stevie, after the album had run itself through, 'a lot of people are expecting this album to be like "Innervisions", which is good, because it's not.

'I've never felt it was good to try to copy the success of something. That just shows you don't want to take a chance. I've taken a chance. I've never liked follow-ups.'

Among the studio visitors that day was Robert Hiburn, who later wrote in *Melody Maker*: 'When just one of his skills [i.e. songwriting, vocal interpretation or arranging] comes through, he has a better than average record. When all of the skills are in peak form, it's a pop masterpiece and he's at that peak form in much of this album.'

' "Innervisions",' said Stevie, 'was a very important album to me. "Visions", for instance, is my very favourite song that I've done up to now. If there is anything I'd like to be remembered by, it's "Visions".

'But this is a very important album too, a very personal one. It was originally supposed to be a double album, but we changed our minds.

'It wasn't that I tried to make it different from "Innervisions", it just turned out that way. My music reflects what is happening in my life and a lot of things happened between "Innervisions" and "Fulfillingness".'

Seven of the ten songs on 'Fulfillingness' were written after the car accident and on this album, as had by now become his habit, Stevie played most of the instruments himself, but there were more guest appearances than usual. Steel guitarist Sneaky Pete was in there, so was the amazing five-octave range voice of Minnie Riperton. The Jackson Five figured too and on one track there was even the voice of pop veteran Paul Anka, who was enjoying hits before Stevie even started his career.

Writing in *Rolling Stone* about 'Fulfillingness', Ken Emerson, abbreviating the title to its initial letters, put, 'FFF concerns the love of God. Wonder's faith has become more inner-directed and other-worldly, less easily threatened by the here-and-now. "Heaven Is Ten Zillion Light Years Away" [one of the song titles] but Stevie Wonder can feel God within him, despite his seeming absence from the contemporary scene.

'A self-assured serenity pervades FFF and it opposes the tension and urgency which made "Talking Book" and "Innervisions" more exciting albums. FFF's tunes and tempo are for the most part easy-going, more like "Sunshine Of My Life" than "Living For The City" or "Superstition". The album aims at relaxed enjoyment; it's not something to get hot and bothered about.

'FFF is less funky, less specifically black than its predecessors. For Wonder's onward and upward development has consistently been away from strict soul music and racial categories or limitations. Because of this, his appeal – greater than that of almost any other performer

73

today – cuts across social and ethnic barriers. In this respect he's ideally suited to Motown, which has never been content with an exclusively black market. But unlike so many Detroit acts, whose wooing of white listeners leaves them pallid and gutless, Wonder's music expands and its integrity is strengthened, not diminished.'

'Fulfillingness' first side opens with 'Smile Please', which was written on the day of the LA Police Department's shoot-out with the SLA. It is a bright, optimistic song, looking forward to better times when violence and social disharmony are things of the past.

'Heaven Is A Zillion Light Years Away', track two, has an instantly memorable melody line, which is one of Stevie's best, and his vocal is full of tenderness. Syreeta Wright and Paul Anka are on backing vocals.

The third track is 'Too Shy To Say', a love song given a slightly country feel by Sneaky Pete's steel guitar work.

Next is 'Boogie On Reggae Woman' which has, as the title would imply, a touch of reggae about it, but its strongest features is a buzzing Moog backdrop. The lyrics are some of Stevie's naughtier ones, for example, 'I like to reggae, But you dance too fast for me, I'd like to make love to you, So you can make me scream!' It was the second single to be taken from the album.

'Creepin'' is a dreamlike ballad and one of the album's lesser tracks. Minnie Riperton sings background vocals.

'You Haven't Done Nothin'' is the first song Motown chose to pull off the album as a single. It's a direct message to US politicians and the album's only out and out rock 'n' roller with all manner of excitement from rending guitar to upfront horns and spirited back-up vocals from the Jackson Five.

'It Ain't No Use' is a rather facile track compared with most of the others. It's a mid-tempo ballad with a pleaant chorus but lyrically rings no new changes on the theme of losing love.

'Bird Of Beauty', is sung partly in Portuguese and was influenced by Antonio Carlos Jobim.

The album's final track is also probably its best. It's called 'Please Don't Go' and moves from lovely simplicity to utter desperation and manages to encapsulate all the various styles Stevie has used in his music.

In the Grammy Awards of 1975 'Fulfillingness' First Finale' was honoured four times, as Album of the Year – Producer; Album of the Year – Artist; Best Pop Vocal performance – Male, 'Boogie On Reggae Woman'; Best R&B Performance – Male, 'Boogie On Reggae Woman'. He picked up a further Grammy Award for 'Living In The City', best R&B song.

CHAPTER SEVEN

Stevie's marriage to Syreeta Wright, a former Motown secretary who became first a back-up and session singer and then a talented singer-songwriter, lasted only eighteen months. When they married in 1970, Stevie was only twenty and had not long left his family home. Maybe at this age and with, perhaps, too much independence too quickly he was not ready for the give and take that marriage requires. At any rate, he admitted after it was all over that he could be very stubborn and that Syreeta, being Leo, which is as strong a sign as Taurus, could be equally stubborn.

Maybe after a while they found themselves at loggerheads too often, but anyway they split up, but without animosity and remain close friends to this day.

After Stevie and his wife separated, Stevie was to be seen mostly with Yvonne Wright (who was no relation to his wife). Yvonne was a Motown songwriter, who hailed from New York and who had co-written several songs with Stevie for his albums.

After a while, he was being seen with a number of different girls, all of them very attractive and some of them connected with Motown.

'I just can't understand it,' confided one of his aides at the time. 'He's permanently surrounded by women. There will be ten women in his dressing room and he picks out the foxiest one every time.'

Stevie says how he does it. 'I can usually tell about a woman by her conversation, her voice and by the way she carries herself. Some women can have a very beautiful outer face and a very ugly inner face.'

After a spell of brief relationships, Stevie soon found a new love. Her name was Yolanda Simmons. The couple have never married. She acts as Stevie's secretary and bookkeeper, as well as being mother to his two children.

Their first-born child was a daughter, Aisha Zakiya, which means life and intelligence. She was born on April 7th, 1975, and it was for her that Stevie wrote one of his best-known recent songs 'Isn't She Lovely'.

Stevie and Yolanda's second child, a son named Keita, was born on April 16th, 1977. The press release put out by Stevie's publicists to announce the happy event was a mixture of formality and jokiness.

'Stevland Morris (AKA Stevie Wonder),' it read, 'and Yolanda Simmons are exceptionally pleased to announce the birth of their first son, Keita Sawandi, on Saturday, April 16th, in New York City. Keita, their second child, weighs 8lbs 7oz, or 3,827 grams, and is 21 inches, or 2,334 cms long. He arrived at 4.10 p.m. on Saturday.' Such detail!

'The baby's name is a combination of West and South African, meaning "Worshipper" and "Founder".'

'Both parents are extremely pleased to have a boy and Aisha is happy to have a brother. Mother Yolanda is recuperating well and father Stevland is as well as can be expected; when last heard from he was resting comfortably!'

Stevie has always said he would like to have a large family 'of fourteen children or more, though I'm not sure I could manage that'. What about poor Yolanda!

For the benefit of those readers who might worry about

such things, it should be said that both Aisha and Keita have excellent sight.

In the course of Stevie's marriage to Syreeta, he produced an album for her. It was commercially unsuccessful, partly perhaps because Stevie refused to publicise the fact that they had made it together. 'People aren't interested in all that husband and wife working together stuff,' he told one journalist at the time.

Syreeta's first album, made soon after Stevie's 'Music Of My Mind', was artistically not much more successful than it was commercially as it was over-arranged and produced and Syreeta's voice got somewhat lost under the might of Stevie's synthesisers.

Long after Stevie and Syreeta were divorced, he produced a second album for her, entitled 'Stevie Wonder Presents Syreeta'. This time nobody was going to miss out on the fact that he had a part in it.

'Stevie Wonder Presents' was a much more successful exercise, allowing Syreeta's voice much more prominence.

The album, co-written by Stevie and Syreeta, was a concept work that might have been written about themselves, since it concerned a love affair that didn't work out.

'A lot of people think the album is about me and Stevie,' said Syreeta, anticipating the question, 'but when I write lyrics I want them to touch on stories. I'm not deliberately writing about Stevie.'

But who could blame people for doubting her when the songs included such titles as ' 'Cause We've Ended As Lovers'.

Some people have dismissed the album merely as pleasant background music, which is unfair, since successful singles were culled from it and successful singles are not made out of background music.

'Your Kiss Is Sweet', Stevie's first attempt at a reggae

song, was a sizeable hit for Syreeta in the UK, while in America she fared well with 'Spinnin' And Spinnin'' and 'I Wanna Be By Your Side', a duet with G. C. Cameron, a former member of the Detroit Spinners. That song came from a suite on the album's second side.

One of Syreeta's best tracks 'Harmour Love' did not get onto the album, but was released as a UK single. The song was heavily influenced by the Brazilian composer Antonio Carlos Jobim. Traces of his style have appeared several times in Stevie's own albums.

'Stevie Wonder Presents Syreeta' was an undoubted success commercially and helped launch Syreeta on her solo career, but there were people who did not like it at all. Duncan Fallowell wrote in *Records and Recording*: 'It's the most awful production/arranging job you could imagine.' On one track in particular, 'I'm Goin' Left', he was even more scathing. 'A leaden pom-pom-pom goes round and round, coming at you through a complete fuzz of mis-echo, distortion, Godknowswhat actually, for honestly I can't disentangle the components responsible for this dreadful noise.'

Doing back-up vocals on 'Stevie Presents' was the redoubtable Minnie Riperton, who had also sung on Stevie's 'Fulfillingness' First Finale'.

Although Minnie is gifted with an incredible five-octave range, it is her high notes that she is best known for, and her voice is one of those that most people either love or hate. I love it, but even her greatest admirers might have doubted the wisdom of her releasing an album.

Stevie, however, reckoned it should be done and, on the album he produced for her, 'Perfect Angel', he wrote in the sleeve notes, 'When Minnie sings I feel my insides rush and quiver. She touches a place in me no-one else

can go. It's hard to believe how incredibly high an
beautiful Minnie can sing.'

The risk of making an album with a voice as unusua
as Minnie's is that it can end up as so much technica
gimmickry and without real feeling. Stevie has alway
said to artists he was producing, 'In singing, emotion i
the main thing.' From Minnie, on those tracks, he got it.

As with Syreeta's first album, Stevie seemed anxiou
with Minnie not to make much of the fact that he was in
volved in the making of the record. He worked on i
under the pseudonym of El Toro Negro (the black bull)
which wouldn't have fooled anybody who knew anything
about Stevie and his birthsign.

In the past few years, Stevie has worked as a produce
with a number of people, among them the Supremes, the
Originals and non-Motown acts like Buddy Miles
Roberta Flack, B.B. King, the Pointer Sisters and Rufus

In the recording studio, Stevie's energy is at its most
phenomenal. Susaye Green, once with his Wonderlove
backing group before she moved to the Supremes, says,
'He has an extraordinary amount of energy when it comes
to music. He is vibrant. I have never known him to sleep.
There were times when we would be working in the
studio and we would leave him there late at night and return early the next morning and Steve would be there still
working where we left him at it. He won't even eat at
times. I guess he must have slept while we weren't
around.'

Stevie points out that not being able to see the change
from day to night can have its advantages. 'My rhythms
go by my moods. I can't tell time by looking outside.
People see nightfall and prepare for it. If my flow is going
I keep on till I peak. Then it's time to move on.'

When a British journalist asked how much of his day

Stevie spent on music, he was told, 'Sometimes it's only half, but others it can be the whole day and into the next,' which bears out what Susaye Green says.

In the studio, Stevie's memory amazes people just as much as his staying power does. Once he was in a studio scatting through a song, when suddenly he stopped, dissatisfied with it and called out to the engineer: 'Erase that.'

'What, all of it?' queried a girl session singer, alarmed that several hours' work was about to be wasted.

'Chile,' he said, turning to her, 'don't think I couldn't do it again.' He seems to be able to remember not only the tune but all the words of every song he ever wrote, including those he gave away. When he mentioned to somebody that Jeff Beck had not done anything with the song 'Thelonius', which Stevie had given to Beck, he said, 'It's too bad,' and sang it straight off.

Even when he is not officially recording, writing or rehearsing, the things he considers essential go with him everywhere – a radio, a cassette player and a small ARP sythesiser at the very least. His hotel rooms always look like upturned musical hardware shops.

Even though he cannot see his surroundings, he has his favourite places. In London he has always stayed at the Royal Garden Hotel in Kensington, although rumour has it he may not be going there again. Apparently last time he was there, his record company in Britain promised to pick up the bill for him and his official entourage, but Stevie had half of his 'non-essential' mates staying there too, for whom Motown declined to pay. Rumour further has it that the Royal Garden are still not entirely happy about the matter.

One writer, watching Stevie in a hotel, was amused to

see that he switched the lights on and off every time he went to the bathroom.

'Everyone else does so,' he was told by an aide, 'so Stevie reckons maybe he should too.'

He is for ever playing practical jokes on people. One evening in London he was watching television with one of his record company personnel.

'That picture's not too good,' complained Stevie, 'would you turn the brightness up a bit?'

The guy was halfway across the room towards the TV contrast switch before he did a double-take and turned to see Stevie convulsed in laughter.

Another time, he was being steered through plate glass doors by two British record company people, who had not had this job before. One of them, so anxious to make sure that Stevie got through safely, cracked his own head against the glass.

'Why don't you look where you're going,' said Stevie poker-faced. 'You blind or something?'

There are many stories about Stevie's sixth sense. One paper even went so far as to say he could detect solid objects up ahead of him by 'acoustical changes' in the air, which does seem rather farfetched. He does, however, manage to pinpoint objects with uncanny accuracy.

One night he was out with his brother Larry. They got out of the car for a walk and Stevie was warned to step over a concrete slab that was in his way, which he did. A few minutes later, he excused himself and went back to the car on his own.

Suddenly Larry remembered the slab and called out to remind Stevie to avoid it, but Stevie was already safely back in the car sitting in the driver's seat.

When Stevie is around, no-one leaves car keys in the

gnition, for one of his favourite tricks is to start the car up and attempt to drive it forward.

Stevie can be very superstitious. He prefers when it is possible for his records to be released at a time favourable to his astrological sign, Taurus, and at times he has been known to board aeroplanes only to get off again and delay his journey 'because the vibes aren't right'.

As with any major star, all kinds of stories have been told about different aspects of his life, but few of them seem well enough grounded to be worth printing. But one of the most intriguing matters for speculation concerns the amount of unreleased Stevie Wonder material in existence. Friends have said that there exist on tape at least two hundred completed, but unreleased tracks, in addition to a whole lot of brilliant live performances.

During the sixties, Stevie recorded a number of things with Eric Clapton, with which both he and Clapton seemed well pleased. It is safe to assume that there are enough Clapton/Wonder tracks in existence to make at least one album, but none of them have ever appeared. Perhaps there was disagreement over them between Clapton's record company and Stevie's, but if that is the case, I've not found anyone who knows anything about it.

A lot of people would also like to know what became of the tracks recorded live on the tour Stevie did with the Rolling Stones in America. Once again, not one of them has ever been released.

In the studio, Stevie works incredibly fast. In one day he may complete rough versions of five or more tracks, only to discard all of them and begin on a fresh batch the following day. In the more recent years of his career, Stevie has become ever more self-critical and perfectionist. For most of his later albums, he has spent a vast amount of time in the studio, recording enough material for perhaps half a dozen albums, before pruning down and weeding out songs until he is left just with those that 'feel right'.

After the car crash, Stevie cut back on his touring schedule to allow him to spend virtually as much time recording as he wanted. Nevertheless, he did manage to put in some brilliant performances on stage.

In April, 1975, Stevie was named the special honoree of Washington D.C.'s annual Human Kindness Day, held each year to celebrate the arts through community involvement. Stevie was given the award on the basis of his 'humanitarian efforts and artistic brilliance' and as a thank you for it, he turned out on May 10th, Kindness Day itself, to climax the proceedings with a free concert for over 50,000 people on the Washington Monument grounds.

The proceeds from Stevie's other American concerts that year all went to charity. He had originally planned to spend some of 1975 in Africa, where he intended to 'start a foundation to find a way to restore the eyes of people blinded by a fungus carried by flies that goes to the cornea of the eye and eats it away', but it was not to be.

On June 12th, 1975, Stevie gave a sold-out benefit performance for the National Newspaper Publishers' Scholarship Fund in San Francisco. The next day he flew back to New York to make a special guest appearance on Geraldo Rivera's annual *One To One* television programme for mentally retarded children, where he sang, answered telephone calls from people who called to pledge money and donated ten thousand dollars himself. Four hours later, he was on his way by plane to Shaw University in Raleigh, North Carolina (near where his car crash had happened).

He served as a member of the University's board of trustees, and during his visit donated money for an elaborate sound system and set up several scholarships. In October of '75, the first plans were laid for the Stevie Wonder Home for Blind and Retarded Children, which was completed in the spring of 1976.

There is no doubt that Stevie's near brush with death helped him realise his own good fortune. He had always been generous with his money, both to his friends and family and to charity. In the months while he was recuperating from his accident, all Stevie's musicians were kept on the payroll, even though he was unable to work.

Once he returned to work after the accident, Stevie's interest in the welfare of people in need became almost a passion. He had already denounced politicians for their lack of concern in song and now he insisted on making his own contribution in practical terms.

His efforts have not been specifically aimed at improving the lot of black people, for, although he has been an articulate spokesman for American black people and their needs, he has always seen all people as equal.

Obviously the welfare of blind people who did not have the same chance in life as himself was of special interest to him, as was the welfare of children. Having recently become the parent of a beautiful healthy daughter, who is the apple of his eye, he was all the more concerned for other children, who were either physically or socially handicapped.

Towards the end of 1975 and in the early months of 1976, he was busy working on sessions for his next album and so public appearances had, of necessity, to be few and far between. He made an appearance on *The Dinah*

Shore Show and was presenter at both the 1975 Grammy Awards and American Music Awards and made a legendary appearance with Bob Marley at the 1975 Supersoul concert in Jamaica.

Kwame Brathwaite, writing in *Blues And Soul*, said of the concert, 'For most Jamaicans and international visitors alike, the main event was the "dream concert" which brought together, for the first time, Stevie Wonder and his group Wonderlove, and Bob Marley and the Wailers and popular reggae group, Third World.

'The concert as promised was fantastic. It will remain one of the gems of soul music, delivering two giants of different areas of black music.'

But not all the notices Stevie Wonder received that year were as enthusiastic. It often happens when an artist reaches the standing that Stevie has achieved that critics get sick of dishing out nothing but superlative plaudits and look for faults to bring the artist down a peg or two.

In 1975 Stevie once again began to play some of the numbers that had made him some thirteen years before. He mostly dished them up as a medley, including such pieces as 'Earth Angel', 'Aint Too Proud To Beg', 'What I'd Say', and 'Fingertips'. Even though crowds at almost every concert yelled out for 'Fingertips', Stevie had not included it in his set for years. Now that he was doing it again, his fans were delighted and roared their appreciation, but the critics greeted the reappearance of such old warhorses with pursed lips. 'They said,' recalls Stevie, 'that I was lowering myself because I was doing all this stuff.'

Still, he was not worried. The crowds who came to his concerts clearly did not agree and Stevie was unbothered by such musical snobbery.

By 1975, Stevie was admired and loved by some of the greatest of his fellow artists, who paid tribute to him by turning up *en masse* at his concerts. He had become close friends with Graham Nash and Stephen Stills and worked with another of America's biggest idols, James Taylor.

Take a listen to them working together on their joint composition 'Don't Be Sad Because Your Sun Is Down', included on James Taylor's 'In the Pocket' album. Their very different styles complement each other exquisitely. Taylor's typically understated, calm vocal is made all the more effective by Stevie's lively instrumental work.

Tributes to Stevie in the form of cover versions of his songs grow ever greater in number, and the following list of just some of them includes a large number of important names and a wide variety of styles.

'You Are The Sunshine Of My Life', one of Stevie's most covered songs, has been recorded by, among many others, Engelbert Humperdinck, Buddy Greco, Andy Williams, Rod McKuen, Sacha Distel, Liza Minelli, James Last, Blue Mink, Perry Como, Ray Conniff, Percy Faith, Johnny Mathis, Frank Sinatra and Petula Clark.

'Superstition' has been done in the widely divergent styles of Mel Torme, The Osmonds, Sergio Mendes and Beck Bogart & Appice.

Ray Charles covered 'Living For The City', along with Maynard Ferguson, Ike & Tina Turner and Ramsey Lewis.

'I Believe (When I Fall In Love It Will Be For Ever)', one of Stevie's most beautiful melodies, has been done by Cleo Laine, Peter Frampton and Art Garfunkel.

Superstars Shirley Bassey and Barbra Streisand both put their stamp on 'All In Love Is Fair', as did Jimmy Helms, Billy Eckstine, Nancy Wilson and Junior Walker, to name only some.

Other people who have recorded Wonder compositions include: Diana Ross and The Supremes, Joan Baez, Tom Jones, Tony Bennett and Bill Cosby. The list seems endless.

CHAPTER EIGHT

In 1975, on the expiry of Stevie's third five-year contract with Motown, he re-signed to the label for a further seven years and for the highest guarantee ever in the history of the record industry. Over the seven-year period of the new contract he was promised earnings of at least thirteen million dollars.

Paul McCartney and Elton John had both recently signed deals with their record companies, which were thought to guarantee them around eight million dollars apiece, and Neil Diamond, shortly afterwards, negotiated a deal that was rumoured to promise him even more, but Stevie's massive new deal left them all standing by several millions of dollars.

It was not the highest offer he received either. Record companies were apparently prepared to lose money to get Stevie unless they had not done their arithmetic correctly. According to Ewart Abner, President of Motown, one rival offer would have meant the record company in question losing a penny on every single copy of every Stevie Wonder record they sold, which, with the numbers of records that Stevie was likely to sell, would have wiped out an oil sheikh.

Robert Hilburn was one of the first journalists to write about the new wonder contract. He reported in the *Los Angeles Times*, 'The contract ends months of speculation that Wonder was unhappy with Motown and would follow the lead of Gladys Knight, the Four Tops and – most recently – The Jackson Five in moving to other labels.

'Thus the re-signing of Wonder is not only important to Motown in terms of the specific retention of the twenty-six-year-old [he was actually twenty-five] singer–song-writer–producer but, indirectly, as a sign to the industry that Motown, despite some charges that the label has been on the decline since its parent company began branching into television and films, continues to have a strong foundation.

'Wonder, who was thirteen when his single "Fingertips" went to number one in 1963 [in America], has been openly critical of Motown at various times during his long association with the label, but he said on Friday that many of his complaints have been corrected and others will be under stipulations worked into the contract.

' "My future is very positive," he said. "There are faults at Motown, but they can be corrected. If you went some-where else, there'd be other problems – probably a lot worse ones. I feel comfortable here. I've known some of the people a very long time. They've let me get away with things that other companies may not have allowed." Albums like "Where I'm Coming From" perhaps?

'In addition, Wonder made it clear that Motown's status as the nation's largest black owned label was a consideration. "My reason also was the fact that I'm a black man," he said, "I'm not a black man who is a racist and I have no hang-up about anybody. I love people for what they are. We can get along and communicate as long as we respect each other. You can be just as easily disrespected by a black man as you can by a white man ... but I'm very proud of my people. I feel that young children – black children – should have something to look up to."

'Though the contract terms were finalised only in the

last two weeks, negotiations between Ewart Abner, president of Motown Records, and Johannon Vigoda, Wonder's representative, began nearly two years ago. Despite some uneasy moments when he would go to one of Wonder's recording sessions and find executives from other labels on hand, Abner remained basically confident that Wonder would re-sign.

'While the negotiations never went into a hard-core bidding arrangement, Abner said that he knew other labels – for reasons greater than simply Wonder's commercial and artistic success – would be willing to pay a record-breaking sum. As the nation's most respected black record-maker, Wonder would be an enormous help to any label trying to create a greater identification with black audiences or desiring to lure more black artists.

'There are companies to whom the acquisition of an artist like Stevland is worth losing money on because of what he might do for them in terms of setting up a chain of events to feed them into another area.' This would explain the bid made by the rival record company, which was prepared to lose a penny a record.

Ewart Abner explained Motown's policy at the outset of the negotiations. 'We made the decision early that we would pay Steve what he could get or better than he could get elsewhere, but for different reasons than the other labels. We recognise who he is and we kind of take pleasure and pride in giving him a contract just for his artistry that is bigger than what others might give to have him as a show piece or as something to attract others.'

The policy of using one huge artist to attract others to a record company can be one of doubtful wisdom. For example, DJM Records had Elton John on their label for years, but were unable to attract anyone who, in commercial terms, enjoyed anything approaching Elton's degree of success. In fact, some artists, in the early stages of their careers, prefer to go to a small new record company finding its way, rather than one dominated by a mammoth artist, where they feel they may become just one of several also-rans.

Ewart Abner's statement at the time of the announcement of the new contract goes to show how, over the years, Motown had learned how to be less secretive about their internal affairs and let the whole world know how their decisions are arrived at. It was one factor which helped Motown to enjoy the enormous respect as a business organisation which it has today.

Abner explained the duration of the contract to the Press and the amount which it guaranteed to Stevie, but he declined to mention the royalty rate that Stevie would be getting from his records. This has been guessed at, however, as being in excess of twenty per cent, against a norm of twelve to fifteen per cent for a superstar artist.

After the signing of the new deal, Stevie said, as well he might, 'This is a good time for me.' Then he added, 'I'm writing a lot of new songs. I've gotten another outlook on life in the last few months. I'm trying to write some songs that get into the essence of knowing what it is like to have a child say "daddy" and to know what it's like as a parent to know when your baby cries that you can feel the tears in your own eyes.'

News of the new deal was greeted with alarm in the British music press, since writers felt that if that kind of money was being promised to artists, in the end it would be joe public that would have to foot the bill in terms of increased record prices.

Perhaps if, as everyone expected, the first album released under the new deal had come out pretty damn quick, the disgruntled murmurings would have been

enced, but delay followed delay and eventually the
murmurings reached a crescendo, culminating in a
lengthy complaint published in the *New Musical Express*,
just before the release of the new album in September,
1976.

The author of the piece, titled 'The Selling Of Stevie',
was Roy Carr, generally one of *NME*'s kindlier writers.
Since what he had to say was indicative of what many
people thought at the time, I quote from it at length.

'Maybe I'm just a cynic,' began Carr, 'but from where
I'm standing it appears that, in terms of pushing as much
product as humanly possible, the thirteen million dollars
Motown Records have guaranteed Stevie Wonder over
the next seven years is far more important than the actual
music that he's expected to deliver in return.

'His figure – Motown have taken great pains to em-
phasise – that's equal to the much publicised deals of
Elton John (MCA) and Neil Diamond (CBS) combined.

'Thirteen million dollars. A king's ransom. But can you
dance to it?! And what kind of record is going to pay the
wage bill?

'Well, after over two years of highly complex contrac-
tual manoeuvring and three cancelled release dates,
"Songs In The Key Of Life" is it – the first of seven instal-
ments in The Biggest Contract In The History Of The
Record Industry – has the dubious distinction of being
the most expensive double album ever released, at a re-
commended retail price of one penny under seven quid.

'"But it comes with a free EP", I hear the man from
marketing utter. Well all I know is that in business,
nothing is for nothing. And at £6.99, it ain't. The way
this particular game has been played gives the distinct
impression that a boardroom stalemate between Wonder
and Motown has been artfully manipulated by everyone

concerned into a sort of ultimate Artistic Superhype.

'Wonder's public have been left to cliffhang for tw[o] years, while young Stevie has been busy getting his thi[ng] together – all thirteen million of it. So has the theo[ry] been, make the punters wait and they'll pay anything?

'Let's get one thing straight: "Songs In The Key [Of] Life" was ready for release at the beginning of the ye[ar] [1976].

'Instead of just scheduling a release date for "Songs [In] The Key Of Life" and honouring that commitment, th[e] powers-that-be could arguably have been utilising ps[y]chological sales techniques by teasing the paying cus[t]omers.

'There've been rearranged unfulfilled deadlines, phot[o]graphs of Stevie sporting a T-shirt emblazoned "We'[re] Almost Ready", and news stories that have given impre[s]sion that the artist was for ever recalling his *Meisterwer[k]* in order to polish it beyond perfection.

'Yet it is common knowledge that some tracks on "Song[s] In The Key Of Life" were recorded before his last albu[m] "Fulfillingness' First Finale", and that following fou[r] separate occasions when the new album had been pr[e]sold to the dealers, orders have now increased to the poi[nt] where the guaranteed advance order is quite probably th[e] largest ever taken. It's well in excess of one millio[n] copies.

'In trying to fully understand the circumstances su[r]rounding the hold-up of "Songs In The Key Of Life", [a] study of the last couple of years reveals many things.

'March 23rd, 1974: *New Musical Express* ran a new[s] story headlined "I QUIT IN '76", in which Stev[ie] Wonder announced that for the next two years he inte[n]ded to tour extensively throughout North America t[o] raise money for charity.

'He further announced that towards the end of 1975 (January 1976 at the latest), he would undertake a farewell world tour, sever all connections with the music business and split to Africa.

'His ultimate destination was to be Ghana – where he would work with handicapped blind and underprivileged children.

'Having lost the Four Tops, Gladys Knight, Martha Reeves, Ashford & Simpson, Holland Dozier Holland, The Detroit Spinners and four of The Jackson Five, Motown were now faced with the imminent departure of their hottest meal ticket.

'So ... a Motown executive wiped the back of his collar and announced: "We shall try to point out to Stevie that he can do more good for the cause by raising money in concert than by going out there to work."

'The subject was never raised again, but it was obvious that all was not well between Wonder and Motown.

'With "Fulfillingness' First Finale" ploughing up the charts, Wonder persuaded Motown to scrap a much-advertised triple "Anthology" package despite the fact the covers had been printed and a number of albums pressed. It was reported that Wonder felt it was more like "Greatest Hits" deal than a representative history of his career.

'Instead, he intimated that a companion to "Fulfillingness' First Finale", entitled "Fulfillingness' Second Finale", was in the pipeline – a double album at that. But it never reached the shops.

'The first half of 1975 was filled with rumours that Wonder was about to leave Motown for another label who were willing to afford him the kind of artistic freedom and cash incentives he desired.

'And Wonder himself made no secrets of the fact that

he was hanging out with such Vinyl Moguls as Cliv
Davis and was prepared to consider any deal.

'When Motown President Ewart Abner dropped in a
Stevie's innumerable recording sessions, he frequentl
found the control booth populated by representatives o
rival labels.' (This bears out what Robert Hilburn had t
say in the *L.A. Times*.)

These representatives, according to Roy Carr, had th
'power and authority to outbid all comers should a
occasion present itself during a coffee break.

'For a time, it looked like Stevie Wonder was set t
become a CBS recording artist, but Motown won in th
end.

'If Stevie Wonder was going to stay with Motown, h
was going to make sure they paid through the nose for hi
services.

'Having bankrolled the deal, Ewart Abner had n
qualms about making it public that Motown had pai
through the nose and made mileage out of the fact.

'Both Abner and Wonder affirmed that a double albun
tentatively entitled "Let's See Life The Way It Is" was or
its way.

'However, it wasn't.

'The next item of gossip suggested that Stevie Wonde
had been advised to nix plans to join Elton John and Th
Beach Boys in the summer of '75 jamboree in London':
Wembley Stadium because he wouldn't get star billing
over Elton. Plans for him to headline a Crystal Palace
Garden Party fell through for different reasons.

'Little else was heard about Stevie Wonder, his album
or the thirteen millions until November 1975. British
promoter Danny O'Donovan let it be known that though
contracts had still to be signed, sealed and delivered, he'd
tentatively scheduled a series of concerts for Wonder in

nuary 1976 at London's New Victoria Theatre – to co-
cide with the release of "Songs In The Key Of Life".
'O'Donovan also lined-up some provincial one-nighters.
mediately, the EMI–Motown reps rushed around the
untry with their order books. But it was a complete
aste of time on everyone's behalf. Neither Stevie nor his
bum presented themselves on these shores.

'After four highly successful albums – "Music Of My
ind", "Talking Book", "Innervisions", "Fulfillingness'
rst Finale" – a clutch of hit singles and ten Grammy
vards, Stevie Wonder became aware of the inherent
ngers of spreading himself thin.

'Though he may have emerged as the most revered
ngle force in black music in the seventies, it was evident
at he had attained his peak at a time when music had
ttle real positive direction. Indeed, it's difficult to esti-
ate the full measure of one's power when almost every-
ing about you is in a continual state of flux.

'Rumours began to filter out of various American re-
rding studios that Stevie Wonder was holding back the
lease of "Songs In The Key Of Life" for as long as
ossible. Aside from the obvious advantage of controlling
oth supply and demand, Wonder was carefully observ-
g whether nostalgia, hard-core disco, salsa, funk, blue-
ed soft soul, reggae, technoflash electronic jazz-rock or
OR was about to dominate the world market.

'Allegedly, Wonder was prepared for any and every
ventuality – to the extent that he'd carefully stockpiled a
uantity of easily-permutated tracks that would encom-
ass every kind of fad or eclecticism. With thirteen
illion dollars and his reputation at stake he had no
esire to be on the tail-end of one bandwagon or to spear-
ead a non-starter.

'Stevie Wonder suddenly scheduled the release for May

10th, 1976 – his birthday. [In fact Stevie's birthday is th
13th.]

'May 10th was extremely important because, accordin
to the singer's personal astrologer, 1976 was a good yea
for Taureans!

'Oh, yes, and "Songs In The Key Of Life" was no
going to be a triple album.

'Immediately, the reps once again flashed around th
world with their order books flapping in the breeze. The
pre-sold more albums than before ... but were unable t
deliver.

'However, now June seemed to be on the cards, 'caus
there was talk of Stevie coming to London on the 5th t
appear at Wembley Empire Pool. Before the touts ha
time to plan their campaign the gig was called off.

'July? Perhaps!

'Photographs arrived of Stevie posing in T-shirts tha
stated either "We're Almost Finished" or "It's Nearl
Finished". Meanwhile, here in London, Motown tried on
more time by distributing T-shirts proclaiming "Stevie'
Almost Ready".

'Having decided that MOR was the thing that sold th
greatest number of units, Stevie Wonder made his fina
selection of tracks, pruned it down to a double plus a fre
EP and aimed his long overdue album straight down th
middle. Not black not white, rather a very serviceabl
grey.

'On Tuesday, September 21st, the media got a previe
and on September 30th your friendly local stockists, wh
between them have ordered 150,000 copies, will b
pleased to do business with you.

'Personally, I can't think of any artist worth thirteen
million dollars or a double album worth £6.99. But lik
the man said, there's a free EP. He did say free, didn't he!

Roy Carr's article gives a remarkable, informed outsider's view of all the mess and confusion that happened between the signing of Stevie's new deal and the eventual release of 'Songs In The Key Of Life', and his story is accurate in all its facts, except for backdating Stevie's birthday by three days, which was a small crime since others have altered it by a year or more.

Naturally Carr's article is slanted against the massive business deal. Part of a music critic's job, apart from informing the public about the artistic merits of records and performances, is to act as a watchdog against the buyers getting ripped-off. It was understandable that Carr should object to a deal which cost the public extra money, just as he was quite within his rights in showing distaste for the way in which Motown capitalised on the album's delay.

All the same, looking at it from the record company's point of view, Motown were in the business of making money, so, for their part, they were quite entitled to whip up enthusiasm and pre-sales for all they were worth until the album finally appeared and, as a business policy, the ploy clearly did work.

One wonders, however, how the lower orders of the Motown hierarchy felt about the succession of delays. Those poor reps scooting round the world taking orders for albums that did not appear must have ended up cursing the name of Stevie Wonder and blowing their tops at sales conferences!

Carr's notion of Stevie sitting on a vast number of tracks waiting to see what music the market would jump for next is an interesting one, since there's no indication of Stevie having done anything of the kind since he came of age.

It seems likely that Carr's theory on this is at least in

part correct. Why otherwise would the album go from double up to a triple and then back down to a doub plus EP?

However, since 'Where I'm Coming From', Stevie ha always been his own man, paying scant regard to wh: was happening around him and putting out music whic he felt was representative of his best work at the time.

It's possible that, having concluded the new dea Stevie felt really nervous for the first time in his caree The thought that every note on an album is worth a b number of dollars could easily shake one's faith in on self and whether one was doing the right thing.

With all the money that was involved, and with all th world-wide publicity, Stevie knew he had to come u with something that sounded worth a fortune, partic larly as, in the eyes of the people who were going to bu it, it actually cost a fortune.

Although Motown managed to bump up advance sale tremendously through the delay of the album, it mu: have cost them a pretty penny to do so, what with all thos reps fruitlessly out flogging non-existent albums, all thos T-shirts and even a whopping great hoarding in th middle of New York, proclaiming the 'almost ready' new

Press coverage, which, of course, cost nothing, did i bit to keep interest buzzing during the long, long wai 'Coming Soon', 'Why Keep Us Wondering?', 'Wonder More Delays' and similar headlines, must have kept th Motown moguls smiling, but I wonder how they took t one in *Sounds* – 'Albums In The Key Of Blunder'.

When the album did at last appear, most people expec ted it to come gift wrapped like there was never going t be another Christmas and so were disappointed with th rather pedestrian cover.

Spencer Leigh, writing in *Blues & Soul*, said: 'It is un

rtunate that the packaging should fall so far behind the
ontents. It was pointless to virtually repeat the outer
over on the inner sleeve and the 24-page booklet would
ave benefited from some photographs and a less high-
row presentation of the lyrics.

'And what's worse is Stevie's enormous self-indulgence
n giving us five pages of credits. Well over 300 names are
n his roll-call and his gratitude is frequently accom-
anied by some cloying remark. (To his parents: "Thank
ou for letting me be your son.")

'There's even a space for you to add your own name so
hat you too are in his dedications. So far I've resisted the
rge to add mine. I seem to remember Pat Boone inviting
s to do the same thing with his book *Twixt 12 and 20*.'

The general opinion of the critics was that the new
lbum was worth the wait. Even the *New Musical Express*
hought so, although they printed the review under the
ryptic heading 'Songs To The Tune Of Seven Quid' and
longside a wicked Tony Benyon cartoon. This, with the
aption 'Almost Finished?' showed an almost skeletal
tevie with sparse beard and moustache and his head
hree-quarters under water.

The headline and cartoon were both ways of getting
back at Stevie for keeping everybody waiting so long, but
they were tempered by the opening paragraph of the
review, which insisted 'Rumours that the *New Musical
Express* has deliberately pursued a course of hostility towards Stevie Wonder are, of course, without foundation'.

This did need to be said, as it was *NME* that dismissed
'Music Of My Mind' as the 'most over-rated album of
'72'. 'Talking Book' was described as 'Better controlled.
However, fifty per cent of it is even more monotonous
than "Music Of My Mind".' 'Innervisions' was dismissed
as 'Far less satisfying than either of the previous two!'

'Fulfillingness' First Finale' feared even worse – 'Grade A Muzak' they called it. However, the *New Musical Express* is renowned for not letting go easily. Once it's got its claws into somebody's album, the next is often 'worse' and the next 'worse still'.

One might think, from reading *NME* cuttings for a year or two, that Stevie Wonder was an artist of no consequence whatsoever, but for 'Songs In The Key Of Life' they were more charitable, spreading their review over an entire page and ending up, 'The music here represents Stevie's most mature work to date. He has cooked up a very rich, and dauntingly expensive, meal. Despite its excellence, I feel that the British public might prefer more bread-and-butter offerings.'

Blues & Soul's Spencer Leigh was less distressed by the price of the album. 'The price has been generally regarded as outrageous, although £6.99 is cheaper than a straight conversion of the American thirteen dollars ninety-eight cents.' That is small consolation, since everybody knows Americans have more money that the average working Brit. Nevertheless, he has better solace in store. 'The package does contain two albums and an EP and, as a single Motown album costs £3.60 the price doesn't seem so exorbitant. What's more,' he adds, as a final *coup de grâce*, 'you can buy it in Boots with £1.50 off.' Bully for Boots.

A lot of critics tended to consider 'Songs In The Key Of Life' as a 'Fulfillingness' Second Finale', a view not shared by *Melody Maker*, whose critic wrote: 'The title of "Fulfillingness' First Finale" suggested that Wonder viewed the work as completion of the initial part of the Grand Design, and so it seemed logical to view "Songs In The Key Of Life" as the start of Chapter Two.'

Melody Maker, which sees itself as being rather more

stablishment orientated than its competitors, is generally
ather sniffy about resorting to the sensationalist tones of
he *New Musical Express,* and thus its review was notice-
bly more restrained in manner and presentation. Under
he heading 'Stevie – a key set', the critic wrote: 'Leaving
side the amusing ballyhoo which preceded the album, it
vill come as little surprise to anyone that Wonder's album
s as accomplished as its five predecessors. The songs, with
ery few exceptions, are excellent, and Wonder's arrange-
nents and production realise them perfectly.'

Around eight meaty paragraphs later, in the course of
vhich he has gone through the album track by track and
nformed us that the EP is 'no throwaway', the reviewer
nds up, 'There are many sides (no pun intended) to
'Songs In The Key Of Life" and not all will emerge to
his listener, I suspect, in the first week or two. All I can
ay is that it is the sort of album which will make you
eplay all your other Stevie Wonder albums. And that's
he best sort of album.'

Sounds, the paper which completes Britain's trio of
veekly music 'heavies', goes for a line somewhere between
MM and *NME,* carrying the headline 'Stevie Delivers.
Was It Worth The Wait? Well ... yes, but ...' and a
victure of Stevie in a cowboy hat, carrying four boxed
albums, with the caption: 'They're a bargain at £6.99 a
hrow, I bought four.'

Sounds' editor, Alan Lewis writes: 'Like the man said:
"If disappointment is inevitable, lie back and enjoy it."'

'After a two-year wait and a "He's nearly finished"
oublicity build-up intended to suggest that this was the
viggest completion job since God downed tools on the
seventh day, there's no way that this album, however
good, can escape the whiff of anti-climax.

'But after six or seven plays (Lewis must have sat up

six or seven nights to get them all in before his deadline enough songs have registered in memory to convince m that it is a far stronger album than his last, even if it fall short of the magnificent "Talking Book" and "Inner visions" albums.

'No radical new directions: most of the songs have their roots on earlier albums. But there are changes. The stri dent sound of the clavinet, which once threatened to be come an almost too dominant trademark of Stevie's work is hardly to be heard. The new toy, used on many of the cuts, is the Yamaha GX10 Electrone Polyphonic Synthe siser, which Stevie refers to as his "dream machine" seem ingly capable of reproducing almost any musical sound ..

'Stevie's singing is probably better on this album than it's ever been. And both vocally and instrumentally, the overall feeling is one of mellow assurance, a man stretch ing out at the peak of his powers.

'But "stretching out", to the tune of two years and several million dollars, is also the album's problem. Every where there's just a bit too much padding. Even some of the stronger cuts outstay their welcome with repetition and lengthy codas. A bit of editing would, at the very least, have made room for the tracks on the "bonus" EP.'

There follows, in parenthesis, yet another swift carp on the expensiveness of the set: 'a curiosity this [the EP]. Was it intended to be a third album? Or was it included to offset the outrageous £6.99 price?'

Lewis also has a go the wordy tome of credits that comes with the package. 'The feeling of excess is height ened by the twenty-four page lyric booklet which, besides a whole lot of elegant white space, includes six pages of credits and acknowledgements, listing everyone from the people who provide the handclaps on the record, to his family (in detail), to the nurses who delivered his baby daughter, and right on down to li'l ol' you and me. Interesting stuff, I suppose, but like other aspects of the album, somewhat overblown.'

After picking his way through the tracks, Alan Lewis concludes: 'The album's worst enemy is its own sense of importance. Get past that biggest-is-best/shrink-wrapped/hardsell/shipped gold/major product/image and you find that once again you are in the warm and caring presence of a master craftsman.'

The national daily press largely echoed what the musical papers had said, but Robin Denselow, writing in the *Guardian*, also had this to say: 'Wonder has succeeded in the seemingly impossible – he has produced highly commercial music that also breaks new ground.

'Wonder uses that limited style, black disco dance music, as a springboard from which to leap off into other musical forms.'

One of the more amusing reviews comes from the specialist publication *Black Echoes*. When writing about black music is your bread and butter, you can clearly not afford to be too carping about its greatest living exponent, so *Black Echoes'* review is understandably effusive in its praise of the new album.

In a general music magazine, there is not usually much argument about who reviews what album, because tastes differ and there's often a natural man for the job, but just imagine what it must be like in the office of a magazine concerned solely with black music when a new Stevie Wonder album arrives after a wait of over two years. One can picture the editor firing warning shots over the heads of the assembled rioters. In this case, the guy who won out in the end, Keith Bourton, writes: 'I wouldn't say there was a battle in *Black Echoes* about who was going to review the set, but if I tell you the rest of the staff will be reading this in hospital ... well ... you get what I mean!'

Although Stevie was accused, along with Motown, of a certain amount of gamesmanship in holding up the release of 'Songs In The Key Of Life', there is no doubt that it caused him many anxious moments and there seems to be some evidence at least that it had an adverse affect on his health.

Maybe he never really took things as easily as he should have done after the car crash, but, at any rate, the *Sunday Times* was moved to write after one encounter with him: 'As a person he is almost frighteningly insubstantial, hardly eating or sleeping, desultorily cared for and strangely alone at the centre of an enormous entourage.'

From what Susaye Green said about Stevie working through the night in the studios, it would appear that he has forsaken his childhood habit of getting a good eight or nine hours sleep per night.

It is also quite likely that he does not eat properly. Since the car accident, he has been a vegetarian, apart from having the occasional piece of white meat, fish or chicken. Stevie has never been a great enthusiast for food and it may be that his near-vegetarian diet does not contain all the nutrients he needs for proper health.

There is no question, however, of him having, as so many musicians do, a problem with either drink or drugs. He drinks very little, even less since the accident than he did before it — just the occasional glass of white wine or maybe a beer.

As far as drugs are concerned, he only once used them, smoking grass just on a single occasion. He said later that the experience frightened him so much that he resolved never to touch it again and has not done so. In fact, he has become very anti-drugs and put down some of his thoughts in his 'Living For The City'.

The reasons why 'Songs In The Key Of Life' did not come out on the many dates it was scheduled to do so have been much publicised, but it is little known why the album came out on the date it finally did. The reason was that it was the last date before the deadline for that year's Grammy Awards, in which obviously Stevie hoped to figure.

'Songs In The Key Of Life' features a large number of guest players, including five guitarists: Mike Sembello, Ben Bridges, Dean Parks, George Benson and W. G. 'Snuffy' Walden. Sneaky Pete returns once again on bass, Nathon Watts plays drums, Raymond Pounds and Gregg Brown help out on keyboards and then there is a large wind section made up of Gregory Phillinganes, Herbie Hancock and Ronnie Foster (horns), Hank Redd (alto sax), Raymond Maldenado, Steve Madaio (trumpets), Trevor Lawrence and Jim Horn (tenor sax), George Bohannon, Glen Ferris (trombones) and Bobbi Humphrey (flute). Then there are percussionists Bobbye Hall, Nastee Latimer and Nathon Afford Jnr. Carmello Hungria Garcia plays timbales and Dorothy Ashby is on harp. You may have heard of very few of them, but it's a wonderful collection of unusual names. In addition to the players, there are background singers too numerous to mention.

All four sides are produced and arranged by Stevie and sides two, three and four are composed entirely by him.

There seems to be no planned structure to the album and it opens with a kind of introduction 'Good morn or evening friends/here's your friendly announcer/I have some serious news to pass on' and you can tell that something fairly pessimistic is coming up. It's 'Love's In Need Of Love Today', a low-key number for an opener. It's followed by 'Have A Talk With God', co-written by

Stevie and his half-brother Calvin Hardaway – 'He's the only free psychiatrist that's known throughout the world.' Then follows one of the album's strongest tracks, 'Village Ghetto Land', where he uses his synthesiser to telling effect behind a chilling lyric, 'Starvation roams the streets/babies die before they're born'. Next is 'Contusion', a jazzy instrumental written after, and inspired by Stevie's accident. The side closes with Stevie's enormously successful single 'Sir Duke', his tribute to the great Ellington.

Side two opens with 'I Wish', another single about looking back on childhood with the lyrics allied to suitably youthful rhythms. 'Knocks Me Off My Feet' is a middle-of-the-road ballad cunningly disguised by a forceful treatment. Even so, the balladeer biggies won't fail to spot its potential for them and cover it in their dozens. 'Pastime Paradise' is next up. Musically it is superb, featuring fantastic percussion, but the lyrics are painfully cliched. 'Summer Soft' is in the same mould as 'Knocks Me Off My Feet'. The side closes with 'Ordinary Pain', which begins as a maudlin love hurts song before developing into something much stronger with Shirley Brewer taking over lead vocal.

Side three opens with 'Isn't She Lovely?' which must be one of the most successful songs ever written by a parent for a child. At the other extreme have a listen to Anthony Newley's 'The Father Of Girls' and you will see how embarrassing parents can be when they start sounding off about their children in song. Despite its title, 'Joy Inside My Tears' is the most dreary track on the whole album, but its follower 'Black Man' is a wonderful rushing thing, although spoilt by a question and answer session between students and teachers played by the Al Fann Theatrical Ensemble of Harlem. It's one of Stevie's all-races-have-done-their-bit-for-America songs.

'Ngiculela – Es Una Historia – I Am Singing' is a gentle samba to open side four and it incorporates Zulu, Spanish and English lyrics. It is followed by 'If It's Magic', which as *Melody Maker* aptly puts it, has Stevie, accompanied only by Dorothy Ashby's rippling harp, managing 'to write convincingly about love for four good verses and two choruses without once mentioning the word'. 'As' is another piece of easy listening which, after its languid opening, shoots into top gear with girl backing vocalists adding to its power. The closing track on this side has a cast of many to make a stirring ending to the album itself. 'Another Star' is a fitting climax to be sure, but there is still the EP to go. It contains a good mixture of styles. 'Easy Goin' Evening' is exactly what the title would have you believe, 'Ebony Eyes' is not the Everly Brothers' song of the same name but one of Stevie's songs that might easily have been written by Neil Sedaka. 'All Day Sucker' is a complicated number harking back to the pessimism of the early part of the album. That leaves 'Saturn', a statuesque piece with a lot of power.

My own opinion of 'Songs In The Key Of Life' is that it shows Stevie at his most mature ever artistically, but too often the songs are allowed to ramble on after the time that should have been allotted to them. If he really had so many songs to chose from, it would have been better if he had shortened some of those that did make it onto the album to accommodate some extra ones that did not. Nevertheless, it remains a powerful work, ranking high among the handful of great double albums which the seventies have produced so far.

Ever since the beginning of the seventies Stevie has been hankering to go to Africa. He often spoke of the fact that a black man should be proud of his identity and his heritage. Although Stevie obviously thinks of himself as an American, he has always had a fascination for Africa. At times he has taken to wearing traditional African clothes and hairstyles. He has also found enough out about African languages to incorporate some of their words in his music. He has even gone so far as to give his children African names.

It was always likely that Stevie would make a trip to Africa and in fact, at one time, it was seriously believed by many that he might give up his recording and performing career to go and live in Africa and set up charities to help blind and underprivileged people there. If he did ever really intend to do this, he was talked out of it by Motown, who told him that he could do far more good by raising money for African causes through his recorded and live work.

However, he still promised himself that he would go there to visit and, after several times putting off the trip, he did finally go in the early part of 1977. His impressions of the country have not yet been recorded in interviews but according to Motown, the experience had a deep effect on him and he is anxious to return again. It is impossible to say when that next visit might be, because all his plans for the future are fluid.

CHAPTER NINE

Today Stevie Wonder has every reason to be a happy man. He has found love of the kind that endures with Yolanda, or Londie as he calls her. He is the father of two children whom he adores. He is a multi-millionaire and has accumulated his wealth through what he likes doing best, making music.

But it could all have been so different. Who knows if he would ever have become a musician if he had not been given that tiny four-hole harmonica off a key chain, and attracted the attention of people through the noises he elicited from it?

He might have been just another blind man from the ghetto, making a living as best he could in some workshop for the handicapped, or, worse still, by begging.

Even when he had acquired the skill as a child to play a wide variety of instruments, his career was nearly, as he put it, 'stopped before it had begun' by the law, which, designed to protect minors from exploitation, made it almost impossible for him, as a twelve-year-old, to appear in public anywhere.

Had one of his playmates not been the brother of Ronnie White of the Miracles, he might never have come to the notice of Motown or any other record company for that matter and ended up simply as one more frustrated amateur musician with talent.

Even when he reached Motown, his future was not

totally assured. Had 'Fingertips' not happened when it did, it was doubtful if Berry Gordy would allow any one of his protégés to make unsuccessful records for long before he dropped them from the label. After all, Motown was a young company which, with the best will in the world, could not afford many failures and certainly not any long-term passengers.

But Stevie's Taurean signs were well-placed and things went right for him – not all the time, but whenever he most needed them to do so.

Even though Stevie's family was forced at times to steal coal to be able to endure the cold of winter when he was a child, he was brought up with a strict sense of what was right and what was wrong, underlined by the puritanical faith of the black Baptist church.

He was, however, no angel as a child. His foul-mouthed cheekiness when he was caught hopping from one shed roof to another was evidence of that.

'I remember,' he recalls, 'when one of my aunts came and caught me doing that and said, "OK Steve, Mama said don't be doin' that," and I said "— you," and some neighbour heard and said, "Aw child, you oughta be ashamed of yourself. I thought you was a child of the Lawd, you out there cussin' n' swearin' 'n' everything."'

As soon as girls became of interest to him, he was off out chasing them down to the local railway tracks, where all the teenage goings-on happened. But for all his youthful exuberance, he was brought up to do right and to be humble, so when his first hits came, he did not immediately let them go to his head. And when the failures came, he did not think the world was at an end in his disappointment. 'Sure I got upset when things didn't go my way,' he said later, 'but not to the point where I ever felt like giving up. Things like that only made me want to try harder.'

Throughout his teenage years with Motown he was not a difficult boy to deal with. He accepted the fact that he had to do schoolwork and got on with it without much complaint. He wrote, played, sang and performed with all the sheer joy of youth and somehow the lure of music never palled.

It was not until he had done everything that his Motown mentors had demanded of him for ten years that he decided finally to cut loose and seek to do things his own way. Even then he chose to stay with the company who had given him his first start. 'Taureans,' he explained, 'do not like change unless it is necessary change.'

It could be said that when he loosened his ties with Motown, Stevie acquired too much freedom too soon and he made the same kind of mistakes that any other young man in the same position might have made. The first album he came up with on his own was a dismal failure, but rather than go running back to the safety of the Motown fold and formula like a prodigal returned, he stuck to what he had begun and made it work – brilliantly – and since then his music has continued to aspire to ever higher peaks.

The marriage he entered into with Syreeta Wright at the age of twenty went wrong after only a short time, but between them, they managed to part amicably and remain firm friends.

The next low spot of his life and probably the most difficult he has ever had to cope with came when he nearly died in a car crash. His courage and will to live and continue his work were so strong that within weeks he was back facing an audience. In many ways, the accident tempered his character and made him more aware, both of other people and of his own gift, which could be used to help others.

He used his music to bring help to people who needed it, but never let his standards drop under the pressure of commitments. As time went on he became more and more painstaking, more and more perfectionist.

At one time he thought of retiring. Maybe the pull of music was too strong to allow him to do that, or maybe he felt that by doing so he would be laying aside the gift God had given him to use, but at any rate, he committed himself to a new seven-year contract, but at a record guarantee of thirteen million dollars' earnings over seven years.

So what of the future? There is no question now of retirement. No record company promises thirteen million dollars in return for nothing and so far, under the new contract, Stevie has produced only one album.

There must be at least three or four albums to come under this present contract with possibly more to follow. It seems unlikely that Stevie would, or could, ever give up writing and recording altogether.

It is likely that his concerts will be fewer and further between. At some point he may give them up altogether, but that does not seem to be on the cards for the immediate future. Motown in America say that he is already talking tentatively about new dates. If they include Britain, they will be his first here since 1974.

One project is now almost definitely set. That is an album for his group Wonderlove, which he has been intending to produce for them for years. In the past, the pressure of his own commitments have prevented him from carrying out that intention, but now things are moving at an easier pace and the Wonderlove album is one of his top priorities.

Moving from the specific to the general, it is impossible

to tell how much further Stevie Wonder can go in terms of artistic achievement. His recent albums have shown only moderate innovation from one to the next, but that may be because he does not feel that he needs to move ahead quite so far as he used to, especially as each new album more than keeps the customers satisfied.

However, when he feels it is necessary, he is not a man to shy away from taking risks, and he is not one for sticking to a formula. The manner in which he felt he had to cut free from the yoke of total direction by Motown proves that.

As a composer, he has new melodies whirling around in his head all the time and there seems to be no possibility that his creative gift will dry up in the foreseeable future. And his fascination with the way that sounds are created remains unblunted. He must still have a gigantic role to play in the development and wider use of synthesisers, which he, almost single-handed, was responsible for introducing into commercial music. His fantastic 'dream machine', used so effectively on his latest album 'Songs In The Key Of Life' may turn out only to be the prototype for something even more fantastic.

As a producer of other people's records, he has been responsible for introducing the public to all kinds of different new music. Would, for example, such excellent groups as Rufus ever have found mass acceptance without his help?

One of the reasons he said he signed to Motown for the fourth time in 1975 was, 'Because they are doing more than any other record company to encourage new black talent.'

It seems certain that, as Motown's most revered and influential artist, he will continue to give a lead to the label's up-and-coming artists and may be responsible, in the last years of the seventies, for introducing us to a whole host of new names and styles of music.

But despite all his many achievements as a musician and the promise he holds in that capacity for the future, perhaps Stevie's biggest contribution to modern society is as an inspiration to people with special difficulties in life.

He has dismissed his own blindness as being no real handicap to him and, by doing so, he has shown people that there is always hope for the future, no matter who you are or how bad things may seem to you. Through his music, he has shown his very real love of humanity and anyone who has had the chance to hear his music and sense that love has responded.

STEVIE WONDER'S CAREER HIGHLIGHTS

1950	May 13th	Born, Stevland Judkins, Saginaw, Michigan.
1961/62		Stevie's playmate, the younger brother of Miracle Ronnie White, heard Stevie playing and was so overwhelmed that he took the child to Motown. Berry Gordy signs the newly named Little Stevie Wonder to a long-term contract with the Tamla label.
1962	August 16th	Release of Stevie's first single 'I Call It Pretty Music (But the Old People Call It The Blues)', featuring Marvin Gaye on drums.
1963	May 21st	Release of Stevie's fourth single 'Fingertips Parts One and Two'.
	May 31st	Release of first album 'Recorded Live – The Twelve-Year-old Genius'.
	June 22nd	'Fingertips Part Two' enters *Billboard*'s Hot 100 and eventually attains number one position.
	August	First release in UK of 'Fingertips' on Oriole CBA 1853.
	August 10th	Receives *Billboard* Award for 'Fingertips'.

	December 26th	Visits England for promotional spots on TV shows *Ready Steady Go* and *Thank Your Lucky Stars*
1964	March 20th	Motown review featuring Stevie Wonder commences UK tour. Acts include Martha and the Vandellas, the Miracles and special guest star Georgie Fame and the Blue Flames.
1965	November 22nd	'Uptight (Everything's Alright)' released in USA.
	December 18th	'Uptight' enters *Billboard* Hot 100 and climbs to number three and tops the R & B charts.
1966	January 14th	'Uptight' released in UK.
	January 21st	Stevie flies into UK for one-nighter tour.
	February 26th	'Uptight' enters UK Top Twenty and reaches number fourteen.
	June 28th	Releases version of Bob Dylan's 'Blowing In The Wind' a subsequent Top Ten hit in America.
1967	May 18th	Releases 'I Was Made to Love Her' which reaches number two in *Billboard*'s Hot 100 and num- five in the UK.
1968	October 15th	Releases 'For Once In My Life' another number two in *Billboard*'s charts and top three entry in the UK.
1969	March 7th	Embarks on eighteen-day UK concert tour.
	May 5th	Meets President Nixon at the White House and is presented

		with the President's Committee on Employment of Handicapped People's Award 'Distinguished Service Award'.
	November 22nd	'Yester Me, Yester You, Yesterday' enters UK Top Twenty and reaches number one giving Stevie his biggest English hit.
1970	January 10th	Awarded 1969 Show Business Inspiration Award by 'Fight for Sight', an organisation promoting research into eye diseases.
	March 16th	First headlining appearances at New York's Copacabana nightclub.
	September 14th	Marries Syreeta Wright.
1971	May 13th	Attaining the age of twenty-one, Stevie receives all his childhood earnings and embarks on the first stage of a new career.
1972	March 3rd	Release of 'Music Of My Mind' in USA.
	May 3rd	Release of 'Music Of My Mind' in UK.
	June 3rd	Supports Rolling Stones on fifty dates from Vancouver to New York.
	November 1st	American release of 'Talking Book'.
	November 25th	'Superstition' tops US soul singles charts.
1973	January 7th	UK release of 'Talking Book'.
	August 3rd	USA and UK release of 'Innervisions'.

	August 6th	Involved in serious car accident in Winston-Salem, North Carolina.
1973	August 18th	'Higher Ground' tops *Billboard* soul charts.
	September 7th	'Innervisions' tops sales of one million in USA.
	September 25th	Makes his first post-accident appearance jamming on 'Honky Tonk Women' with Elton John at Madison Square Gardens, New York.
1974		Stevie sells out all concerts at London's Rainbow in his most recent UK appearances to date. Presented with five Grammy Awards in the following categories: Album of the Year: Producer – 'Innervisions'. Album of the Year: Artist – 'Innervisions'. Best Pop Vocal Performance – Male – 'You Are The Sunshine of My Life.' Best R&B Male Vocal – 'Superstition'. Best R&B Song – 'Superstition'.
1975		Presented with five Grammy Awards in the following categories: Album of the Year: Producer – 'Fullfillingness' First Finale'. Album of the Year: Artist –

120

'Fullfillingness' First Finale'.

Best Pop Vocal Performance Male – 'Boogie on Reggae Woman'.

Best R&B Performance Male – 'Boogie on Reggae Woman'.

Best R&B Song – 'Living For The City'.

1975 Re-signed to Motown with a multi-million-dollar contract – largest ever negotiated in recording history.

Performing in Jamaica with Bob Marley and the Wailers.

Birth of daughter Aisha.

1976 September 30th Release of 'Songs In The Key of Life'.

1977 Birth of son Keita.

Visit to Africa.

STEVIE WONDER DISCOGRAPHY

UK SINGLES

Fingertips Part Two 8.63
Workout Stevie Workout 11.63
Castles In The Sand 4.64
Hey Harmonica Man 8.64
Kiss Me Baby 3.65
High Heel Sneakers 9.65
Uptight (Everything's Alright) 1.66
Nothing's Too Good For My Baby 4.66
Blowing In The Wind 8.66
A Place In The Sun 12.66
Travellin' Man 3.67
I Was Made To Love Her 6.67
I'm Wondering 10.67
Shoo-Be-Doo-Be-Doo-Da-Day 4.68
You Met Your Match 8.68
For Once In My Life 11.68
I Don't Know Why I Love You 3.69
Yester-Me, Yester-You, Yesterday 11.69
Never Had A Dream Come True 3.70
Signed, Sealed, Delivered (I'm Yours) 6.70
Heaven Help Us All 10.70
We Can Work It Out 5.71
Never Dreamed You'd Leave In Summer 7.71
If You Really Love Me 1.72
Superwoman 9.72

UK ALBUMS

0352	Star	
	General	*(all are illustrated*
396865	Margaret Duchess of Argyll **FORGET NOT**	70p
398078	The Duchess of Bedford **NICOLE NOBODY**	75p
300485	Helen Cathcart **ANNE AND THE PRINCESSES ROYAL**	75p
397004	Tommy Cooper **JUST LIKE THAT!**	50p
39854X	Paul Dunn **THE OSMONDS**	80p
397071	Margot Fonteyn **MARGOT FONTEYN**	75p
396601	Gerold Frank **JUDY (Large Format)**	£1.95p
300299	Noele Gordon **MY LIFE AT CROSSROADS**	50p
398108	Brian Johnston **IT'S BEEN A LOT OF FUN**	60p
396873	Renee Jordan **STREISAND**	75p
39644X	Hildegarde Knef **THE VERDICT**	95p
398841	Vera Lynn **VOCAL REFRAIN**	60p
300973	Ralph Martin **THE STORY OF THE DUKE AND DUCHESS OF WINDSOR. THE WOMAN HE LOVED**	95p
397039	Jessie Matthews **OVER MY SHOULDER**	60p
398396	Pat Phoenix **ALL MY BURNING BRIDGES**	60p
397578	Raymond **RAYMOND**	75p
396806	Brian Rix **MY FARCE FROM MY ELBOW**	75p
397497	John Stonehouse **JOHN STONEHOUSE — MY TRIAL**	95p
398876	Charles Thompson **BING**	70p
398264	Peter Underwood **DANNY LA RUE: LIFE'S A DRAG**	55p
397268	Mike and Bernie Winters **SHAKE A PAGODA TREE**	60p
398302	Mike Yarwood **AND THIS IS ME!**	50p
300000	**ERIC AND ERNIE: THE AUTOBIOGRAPHY OF MORECAMBE & WISE**	50p

*Not for sale in Canada.

GENERAL NON-FICTION

0352   Star

396431	Frederick Anderson **ENGLAND BY BICYCLE**	95p
398914	J. Paul Getty **HOW TO BE RICH**	60p*
397829	**HOW TO BE A SUCCESSFUL EXECUTIVE**	60p*
397152	Nick Logan & Bob Woffinden **THE NME BOOK OF ROCK 2**	95p
398566	Harry Lorayne & Jerry Lucas **THE MEMORY BOOK**	60p*
39692X	Henry Miller **THE WORLD OF SEX**	60p
396407	Milligan & Hobbs **MILLIGAN'S BOOK OF RECORDS**	75p
396733	Sally O'Sullivan **THINGS MY MOTHER NEVER TOLD ME**	85p
397640	David Reuben **HOW TO GET MORE OUT OF SEX**	85p*
398779	Fiona Richmond **FIONA**	50p
300213	Ernest Tidyman **DUMMY**	45p*

0426   Tandem

181123	Eppstein (Editor) **THE BOOK OF THE WORLD**	£1.75*
08571X	Hyam Maccoby **REVOLUTION IN JUDAEA**	75p
163877	James Hewitt **ISOMETRICS AND YOU**	40p
168623	Xaviera Hollander **THE HAPPY HOOKER**	60p*
163443	**LETTERS TO THE HAPPY HOOKER**	60p*
168038	**XAVIERA GOES WILD**	75p*
166787	**XAVIERA, ON THE BEST PART OF A MAN**	60p*
17996X	Xaviera Hollander & Marilyn Chambers **XAVIERA MEETS MARILYN CHAMBERS**	60p*
124820	Charles Lindbergh **THE SPIRIT OF ST. LOUIS**	95p
124901	Fridtjof Nansen **FARTHEST NORTH**	£1.00
175158	Sakuzawa Nyoiti **MACROBIOTICS**	50p*
181204	L. Sprague De Camp **ANCIENT ENGINEERS** (large format)	£1.95*
134931	**THE WOMANLY ART OF BREAST FEEDING**	60p

*Not for sale in Canada.

0352		Star	
30006X	THE MAKING OF KING KONG B. Bahrenburg		60p*
398957	THE MARRIAGE RING("COUPLES") Paddy Kitchen & Dulan Barber		60p
397276	MURDER BY DEATH H. R. F. Keating		60p*
398825	McCOY: THE BIG RIP-OFF Sam Stewart		50p*
398035	PAUL NEWMAN Michael Kerbel		75p
397470	ODE TO BILLY JOE Herman Raucher		60p*
398191	THE ROCKFORD FILES Mike Jahn		50p*
397373	THE SCARLET BUCCANEER D. R. Benson		60p*
398442	THE SIX MILLION DOLLAR MAN 3: THE RESCUE OF ATHENA ONE Mike Jahn		45p*
398647	THE SIX MILLION DOLLAR MAN 4: PILOT ERROR Jay Barbree		50p*
396490	SIX MILLION DOLLAR MAN 5: THE SECRET OF BIGFOOT Mike Jahn		60p
396652	SPACE 1999: (No. 2) MIND BREAKS OF SPACE Michael Butterworth		60p
396660	SPACE 1999 (No. 1) PLANETS OF PERIL Michael Butterworth		60p
398531	SPANISH FLY Madelaine Duke		50p
398817	SWITCH Mike Jahn		50p*
398051	THE ULTIMATE WARRIOR Bill S. Ballinger		50p*
0426		Tandem	
180240	AT THE EARTH'S CORE Edgar Rice Burroughs		50p
180321	THE LAND THAT TIME FORGOT Edgar Rice Burroughs		50p
164164	LENNY Valerie Kohler Smith		50p*
16184X	ONEDIN LINE: THE HIGH SEAS Cyril Abraham		60p
132661	ONEDIN LINE: THE IRON SHIPS		60p
168542	SHAMPOO Robert Alley		50p

*Not for sale in Canada.

0352   Star

396881	**A STAR IS BORN** Alexander Edwards	60p
396792	**THE BIONIC WOMAN (No. 1)** **DOUBLE IDENTITY** Maud Willis	50p*
39689X	**BIONIC WOMAN (No. 2)** **A QUESTION OF LIFE**	50p*
398175	**THE BLACK BIRD** Alexander Edwards	45p*
398256	**CANNON: THE FALLING BLONDE** Paul Denver	50p*
398728	**CANNON: IT'S LONELY** **ON THE SIDEWALK**	50p*
396687	**CARQUAKE** Michael Avallone	60p
397349	**COLUMBO: ANY OLD PORT IN A STORM** Henry Clement	50p*
398183	**COLUMBO: A CHRISTMAS KILLING** Alfred Lawrence	45p*
300795	**COLUMBO: THE DEAN'S DEATH**	40p*
30099X	**DIRTY HARRY** Phillip Roch	60p
396903	**EMMERDALE FARM (No. 1)** **THE LEGACY** Lee Mackenzie	50p
396296	**EMMERDALE FARM: (No. 2)** **PRODIGAL'S PROGRESS** Lee Mackenzie	60p
397489	**ESCAPE FROM THE DARK** Rosemary Anne Sisson	50p
398744	**GABLE AND LOMBARD** Joe Morella & Edward Z. Epstein	60p*
397160	**HARRY & WALTER GO TO NEW YORK** Sam Stewart	50p*
398493	**HAWAII 5-0: THE ANGRY BATTALION** Herbert Harris	50p*
300876	**HAWAII 5-0: SERPENTS IN PARADISE**	45p*
396288	**HEAVEN HAS NO FAVOURITES** Erich Maria Remarque	75p
398477	**HUSTLE** Stephen Shagan	60p*
398574	**INNOCENTS WITH DIRTY HANDS** Richard Neely	60p*
397500	**INSERTS** Anton Rimart	60p
397438	**KOJAK: GIRL IN THE RIVER** Victor B. Miller	50p*
397357	**KOJAK: GUN BUSINESS**	50p*
397446	**KOJAK: MARKED FOR MURDER**	50p*
398671	**KOJAK: TAKE-OVER**	50p*

*Not for sale in Canada.

Wyndham Books are obtainable from many bookse
and newsagents. If you have any difficulty please s
purchase price plus postage on the scale below to:

Wyndham Cash Sales
44 Hill Street
London W1X 8LB

While every effort is made to keep prices low, it is so
times necessary to increase prices at short no
Wyndham Books reserve the right to show new
prices on covers which may differ from those advert
in the text or elsewhere.

Postage and Packing Rate

U.K. & Eire
One book 15p plus 7p per copy for each additional
ordered to a maximum charge of 57p.

These charges are subject to Post Office charge fluc
tions.